Through this absorbing, keenly observed study of Senegal's culinary landscape, Pierre Thiam has painted a beautifully rendered portrait that highlights the countless shades and textures of one of our world's most enduringly vibrant cultures. Both touchingly reverent and arrestingly modern, this book gave me a profound appreciation for Senegalese cuisine and the richly diverse people who have created and sustained it.
— LEE SCHRAGER, AUTHOR OF *FRIED AND TRUE*

Pierre Thiam is a New York culinary treasure, having done more to popularize West African food in the city than anyone else, first as a chef, then as a cookbook author. This, his second published effort, is nearly as good as a trip to Dakar, filled with stunning color photos and great recipes.
— ROBERT SIETSEMA, AUTHOR OF *NEW YORK IN A DOZEN DISHES*

Pierre Thiam brings his native Senegal to life visually and verbally through its food traditions and history. Pierre shows us the many foods of Senegal, from ancient dishes that eventually were copied all over the globe to more modern ones stemming from immigrants of other former French colonies, Lebanon and Vietnam. Reading this cookbook, which is remarkably pertinent to current modern foodways as the traditions are based on farm to table, makes me want to hop on a plane for Dakar tomorrow to explore for myself this fascinating cuisine and country.
— SARA JENKINS, AUTHOR OF *OLIVES AND ORANGES*

This book transports you directly to Senegal. I can almost smell the food rising from the beautifully sensitive photographs. The book captures the wonderful cultural vibrancy of the Senegalese people and their cuisine.
— DANNY SIMMONS, ARTIST AND CREATOR OF HBO'S *DEF POETRY*

Senegal is a significant and timely contribution to the culinary literature of Modern Africa. Chef Pierre Thiam has again given us a taste of the exquisite riches of the Senegalese kitchen that I grew up loving. **— AKON**

TO MAMAN
AND PAPA,
AND TO
RANDY
WESTON

LAKE ISLE PRESS, Inc.
New York

SENEGAL

MODERN SENEGALESE RECIPES

>>>•>>> FROM «<•<<<

THE SOURCE
TO THE BOWL

PIERRE THIAM

WITH JENNIFER SIT

Published by:
Lake Isle Press, Inc.
2095 Broadway, Suite 301
New York, NY 10023
(212) 273-0796
E-mail: info@lakeislepress.com

Distributed to the trade by:
National Book Network, Inc.
4501 Forbes Boulevard, Suite 200
Lanham, MD 20706
1(800) 462-6420
www.nbnbooks.com

Library of Congress Control Number:
2015930449

ISBN-13: 978-1-891105-55-5
ISBN-10: 1-891105-55-8

Book and cover design:
Laura Palese

Map design (page 32):
Haisam Hussein

Co-writer/editor: Jennifer Sit

This book is available at special
sales discounts for bulk purchases
as premiums or special editions,
including customized covers. For
more information, contact the
publisher at (212) 273-0796 or by
e-mail: info@lakeislepress.com

First edition
Printed in China

10 9 8 7 6 5 4 3 2 1

CONTENTS

FOREWORD

BY JESSICA B. HARRIS

I journeyed to West Africa for the first time in 1972, the year that Pierre Thiam turned seven years old. I was going to do research for my doctoral dissertation on West African theatre and had mapped out an extensive itinerary that would take me throughout the region. A last-minute glitch meant that my mother became my traveling partner and the die was cast for a trip that would announce a lifelong fascination with Senegal and its food.

Arrival at the Dakar airport signaled my entrance into a world that was at the same time wondrous and *exotique*, yet somehow comfortingly familiar. With my mother as co-conspirator, we ventured into the world of a Senegal in which Americans, especially Black Americans, were the exception, indeed exotic in our own way. Those were the days before *Roots*, the book and television miniseries that transformed relationships between Africans and ourselves.

In the course of our stay, we visited the capital and were invited into homes by folks we'd only just met—evidence of the legendary Senegalese hospitality or *teranga*. There we learned to eat from traditional communal bowls with our right hands, patiently waiting for morsels to be distributed into our quadrants by the premier lady of the household.

We visited the city's main markets: Kermel, where the Europeans shopped; Sandaga, where one could purchase everything from a goat on the hoof to gold jewelry; and Tilene, where many locals purchased ingredients for their daily meals. We journeyed to Cayar and braved the flies and funk to watch as fish were split and sun-dried on wooden tables. Most of all we ate, savoring the culinary variety that the country offered and still offers. We sampled the hibiscus flower drink known as *bisaap rouge* and discovered the surprising laxative qualities of *dakhar*, a marvelously refreshing tamarind drink. At every turn we were astounded by the diversity of the nation's food, by its multiple influences, and by its just plain deliciousness.

Pierre Thiam is Senegal's ambassador for that food—the same food that I first tasted more than forty years ago and the food that he grew up with. Pierre was fortunate to have been born into a family with a rich culinary tradition, a tradition that inspires his current work as a top chef of Senegalese cuisine.

The book you are now holding—*Senegal: Modern Senegalese Recipes from the Source to the Bowl*—is a passport into a culinary realm that is at once traditional and innovative. American Southerners will discover hints of New Year's Hoppin' John and the familiar slip of an okra gumbo. However, all is not familiar. There are the new tastes of smoked mollusks and the rediscovery of ancient grains such as fonio. Like *Yolele!*, Pierre Thiam's first cookbook, this work is a journey into a culinary universe that is rich and ripe for exploration. Walk with him through the pages of *Senegal: Modern Senegalese Recipes from the Source to the Bowl* and enter the world of Senegal: its people, its culture, and most importantly, its food.

PREFACE

The African continent has one of the richest diversity of cultures in the world. With over fifty countries and an estimated 2,000 languages spoken, Africa has multitudes to offer and yet the many cuisines of the continent remain relatively unknown. Unbeknownst to many, African cooking is rich, soulful, and complex, and West Africa in particular is a profound contributor to the global culinary world. From staple ingredients such as rice, okra, and sesame, to pots full of gumbo or rice and beans, a quick glance at the foods of the Americas and the African diaspora can attest to the indelible impact the continent has had on how we eat today.

There has been perhaps no other time when eaters around the world are as curious, adventurous, and ready to discover new tastes and experiences, and I believe that African foods are poised to join the table in a significant way. As a Senegalese chef, I begin with Senegal, of course, but there are many other cuisines to discover, each with its own unique soul and flavor: from the deeply verdant *ndolé* stews of Cameroon to the peanut-dusted grilled lamb skewers of Nigeria, Africa is rich with gastronomic possibility. Many will find the tastes of the African continent surprisingly familiar, a muted exoticism that only further underlines the deep-rooted influence of well-traveled ingredients and cooking techniques. There are many stereotypes and misconceptions surrounding Africa and its people, and the foods we eat are only a small part of it. Africa is no single homogeneous country, and of all its beautifully diverse identities and cultures, Senegal is but one.

I hope that the readers of this book come away understanding the depth of this cooking and its place in the world so that it is no longer unfathomable, alien, misunderstood—not just forgotten, but unseen. When I say readers, I mean both non-African and African, because one of the enduring tragedies of colonialism is that Africans were conditioned to believe that everything from the West is better, that to be native is to be inferior. As the world once again looks to Africa as a continent of economic opportunity, it's more important than ever that we understand there is so much more to be offered than just minerals and resources, that Africa is not defined by what can be taken, reaped, exploited. We must bring light and pride to the undervalued. We must realize that our food is good enough to be shared with the world, that food does not have to be complicated or precious to be good, that it can be full of our soul, our love, authentic and true to our history and identity—a pure and always delicious thing.

INTRODUCTION

This book is a quest for and a tribute to the roots of Senegal's rich, multifaceted cuisine. We will travel from the northern colonial city of Saint-Louis, a fishing city and former French colonial capital perched at the edge of the Sahara desert and bordering Mauritania, where the Senegal River meets the Atlantic Ocean; then south to the tropical palm forests of Casamance, where the warm rains feed traditional rice paddies and the mangroves abound with oysters. To the east, we'll travel along the Gambia River that bisects the country to Kedougou, the foot of Guinea's Fouta Djallon highlands, green and lush, home to the ancient grain *fonio*. Along the coast, curving outward into the Atlantic and converging in a pinch, is the African mainland's most western point, Senegal's largest city and capital: the bustling, sun-bright Dakar. The food scene of Dakar, Senegal's melting pot, emits flashes of French, Lebanese, and Vietnamese, traces of its colonial history that stand alongside the neighborhood restaurants serving the foods of Senegal's West African neighbors who have settled here for many generations, now more than ever.

Along the way, you'll meet local farmers, fishermen, humble food producers, and home cooks each with a story to tell, techniques to teach, recipes to share and savor. Some dishes may seem comfortingly familiar but remain distinctly Senegalese, such as a bright salad of grapefruit, avocado, and cashew nuts, ingredients that will take you to the shaded fruit trees of Casamance; or cassava leaves, usually found in traditional stews, made into a bold pesto that you'll want to slather on just about everything; or a lamb leg seasoned with thyme, cumin, garlic, and Dijon, slowly roasted until the meat falls off the bone as is done at my favorite Dakar *dibiterie*. Other dishes will introduce you to techniques, flavor combinations, and ingredients that will be new and exciting to discover, such as *moringa*, a green plant also known as *nevedaye* (sounds like "never die") that possesses super health properties, or *fonio*, an ancient whole grain, small and couscous-like, that is gluten-free and highly nutritious—in other words, poised to take over quinoa as the next healthy it-food.

My first book, *Yolele!*, was the first Senegalese cookbook ever to be published in the English language. The recipes in *Yolele!* reflect my personal journey, encompassing travels throughout West Africa, Europe, and finally New York City, which I now call home. *Yolele!* allowed me to reach a whole new audience, and I've found myself becoming a sort of culinary ambassador, traveling the world to spread the good news about African food. I am so proud of that book and its significance, but I felt that my job was not done. *Yolele!* introduced Senegalese food to the world; this book will take a deeper dive, showcasing ingredients and techniques elemental to Senegalese cooking, the food producers at the heart of its survival, and the cultural and historical context it exists in. This is the food of Senegal, from the source to the bowl.

MY STORY

I was born and raised in Dakar, a bustling city on the west coast of Africa. On a peninsula, it is the most western point of the African continent, and the weather always seems perfect with pleasant breezes and unfailingly blue skies.

Growing up, I spent my summer holidays in Ziguinchor, the capital of Casamance in the southern part of Senegal. Compared to the dusty desert climes of northern Senegal, Casamance is a tropical dream, lush and fertile with abundant rainfall. Casamance is in fact the "food basket of Senegal" where rice, millet, *fonio*, peanuts, and many tropical fruits are grown. My parents grew up in Casamance, where my grandparents had a family compound. My grandfather raised pigs, and my grandma let chickens and ducks range free in her vast backyard. Their garden was full of fruit trees: coconut, mango, tangerine, and papaya, just to name a few. Raising chickens and growing vegetables in your backyard are common practices in Senegal, and in Grand-Mère's garden, she tended to okra, bitter eggplant, Scotch bonnet peppers, corn, and sorrel.

After graduating high school, I studied physics and chemistry at Cheikh Anta Diop University in Dakar. During my second year, in the late eighties, a series of protests that grew to become the now-infamous *Année Blanche* interrupted the Senegalese school year. The country was going through a period of turmoil, and the government shut down the universities and all public schools because of the political tensions fomented there. Students in Senegal are very opinionated, and protesting is one common way to express frustration with the system. Since the schools were closed and the year was declared "blank" and would not count, I had no other choice but to face my destiny, which meant leaving Senegal for my education. Luckily, I applied to and was accepted at a small college in Ohio and another chapter of my life was to begin.

I arrived in New York with a student visa in the fall of 1989. New York was only meant to be a short stop on my way to school in Ohio, but a set of circumstances decided otherwise, and a quarter of a century later, I'm still here in New York, never having made it to Ohio. Upon arriving in New York, I instantly felt like I belonged. I got my first restaurant job and realized that my true calling was for a kind of chemistry different from the one taught in the university labs. I have lived here ever since, now with Umaimah, my life partner, and Sitoë, Elijah, and Haroun, our three children born right in our Brooklyn home.

Having now spent equal amounts of my lifetime on both sides of the world, I consider myself a product of Dakar and New York. One of the founding fathers of Senegal, the poet-president Léopold Sédar Senghor, envisioned the "Universal Civilization" to be the day when the "Rendezvous of Giving and Receiving" will take place. I humbly feel that his emphasis on cultural hybridism, a new universality that corresponds to diverse cultures and experiences rather than solely Western ones, is the story of my life. I've received much from my New York experience and have always felt that my duty is to give back by sharing with the West the food culture of my native Senegal in particular and of Africa in general.

When I wrote my first cookbook, *Yolele!*, my Brooklyn restaurant, Le Grand Dakar, was a cultural center dedicated to introducing the food culture of West Africa to the Brooklyn community. Sharing culture through food has always been my driving passion and *Yolele!* was written in that spirit. It is a tribute to the women of my family (and by extension, the women of Africa), who inspired most of the primarily traditional recipes in the book.

Since closing Le Grand Dakar, I have become a sort of roving food ambassador, traveling the world to spread the word about the values of our cuisine. I continue to run my catering and event-planning business, give lectures and cooking classes, and consult in the restaurant industry. I've also begun working with some of my favorite Senegalese producers to import, package, and distribute their amazing products in the United States. They are the foods I grew up eating and I'd love to share them with the world.

LES SÉNÉGALAIS AND THE VALUES THAT BIND

Senegal, a tolerant and relatively peaceful country, is made up of over ten ethnic groups, with the Wolof people living in the northwest and central regions of the country forming the majority. Regardless of one's ethnicity, Wolof is the most widely spoken language throughout Senegal. French is the official language but only a minority formally educated through the school system speak it fluently. Other major ethnic groups, each with their own spoken language, are the Fulani in the north and south, the Serer in the central region, the Bassari in the southeast, and the Diola and Mandingo in the south. Wolof as a common language is indeed a formidable unifying tool across all ethnic groups, and many regions are in fact ethnically diverse. As is the case in most African countries, the borders that demarcate the regions of Senegal are purely an administrative product. Although Senegal is largely peaceful, there does exist a low-level civil war that has been waged by a movement for the independence of Casamance since 1990. It's similar to the Basque and the Corsican movements in Spain and France. Ongoing discussions and recent developments lead me to believe that things are evolving toward a peaceful resolution.

In addition to the native Senegalese, there is a significant immigrant population. A small Lebanese community has lived in Senegal for many generations now, and is very much part of the social fabric. In terms of food culture, their touch can be seen in the popularity of late-night shawarma joints and *fataya*, a widely popular snack consisting of fluffy bread bundles stuffed with spiced beef and mint.

A smaller group of Vietnamese people migrated to Senegal around the time of the First Indochina War while Vietnam and Senegal were both still under French colonial rule. The Vietnamese arrived at the heels of the French colonial army, the *Tirailleurs Sénégalais* that mostly consisted of Senegalese soldiers. The refugees had fled an embattled Vietnam, which was at the time engaged in a fierce war for independence. Among the refugees was Tonton Jean, my godfather and the man who was to become one of the major inspirations in my career choice as a chef. In Senegal, the kitchen is a sacred domain that belongs to women and Tonton Jean was the first man I had ever seen cooking while I was growing up. Seeing him whipping up his culinary magic and serving amazing Vietnamese dishes remains one of my most intriguing yet fondest food memories. Like the French and Lebanese before them, Vietnamese expats brought their cuisine to Senegal and the Senegalese embraced it. It is all so ingrained that even today, it's very common to find Senegalese eateries serving ethnic fare from these countries, and there can be no traditional celebration without *nems* (Vietnamese spring rolls) or Lebanese *fataya* on the menu.

Despite the cultural differences that may exist from one place to another, we've been able to stay united and, for the most part, remain a peaceful country. The strength of social cohesion in Senegal is partly due to what is commonly called the *parenté à plaisanterie*, which translates to "kinship pleasantry." This ancient West African tradition, known as *kal* in Wolof, is still very much alive in Senegal. Kinship pleasantry allows members of different ethnic groups to jokingly criticize others without a hitch, a relationship that may also take place between families. Thus a Thiam family member could accuse a Sow or a Sarr family member of being a glutton or a big rice eater without anyone being shocked. It is always in good fun as sometimes the individuals don't even know each other at all. Situations can be pretty comical as no one is allowed to take offense. This lighthearted relationship creates a common heritage and contributes to reducing interethnic problems, making the Senegalese society a tolerant nation of peaceful coexistence.

It is believed that the name "Senegal" comes from the local Wolof word *sunugaal*, which means "our dugout boat." The meaning suggests that we all share the same dugout boat so we ought to be careful not to capsize it. Across the country, we share a common set of values that help us achieve that peace and stability, and much of that is embodied in our sense of *teranga*, meaning "hospitality." *Teranga* teaches us to have a high regard for strangers and guests alike who are always welcome to share a meal. No matter the ethnicity, we are bound by traditional values of *kersa* (respect for others), *tegin* (good manners), *mbokk* (a strong sense of family), *fayda* (determination), *jomm* (belief in one's self), and *mougn* (patience). These are our guiding principles, many of which are expressed in the way we share our food, welcoming others to sit around the bowl and eat.

SENEGAL AND THE NEW WORLD

As with jazz music, Africans who came to the Americas as slaves used their intuition to recreate African food everywhere they went. From the Lowcountry cooking of the American South to the sophisticated cuisine of Bahia, the soul of Brazilian food, the culinary influences are unapologetically African. Major ingredients such as black-eyed peas, okra, sesame, and watermelon, to name a few, first arrived in the Americas through the transatlantic slave trade.

The Carolina Gold rice that made South Carolina one of the wealthiest colonies was the African *Oryza glaberrima* from Senegal brought by captives who were experts in rice cultivation. Of course with African cooks in the New World kitchens as well, rice-based dishes were plentiful. Variations of Senegal's *thiebou niébé*, a dish of rice and black-eyed peas, show up everywhere: it became the Hoppin' John of South Carolina, rice and peas in Jamaica, *pois et riz collés* in Haiti, *moros y cristianos* in Cuba, *jambalaya au congri* in Louisiana, and *feijoada* in Brazil. In the Gullah Islands, the same red jollof rice of Senegal's *thiebou jenn* remains very popular today.

The "Africanization of the New World palate," as scholar and cookbook author Jessica Harris puts it, did not stop there. Jessica has done more than anyone to further our understanding of the foods of the African diaspora. In her work, *The Welcome Table: African-American Heritage Cookbook*, Jessica writes of the "culinary tendencies that traveled from Africa to America and are emblematic of African-inspired cooking in the United States and indeed throughout the hemisphere," including the addition of smoked meat and fish to stews and soups as seasoning; the use of okra, nuts, and seeds as thickeners; the abundance of fritters indicative of West African deep-frying techniques; the adoption of hearty rice dishes and leafy greens; and lastly, the generous use of spicy hot pepper sauces.

Examples of Africa's contributions to dishes around the world abound. There is Senegalese *soupou kandja*, a seafood-okra stew from which Louisiana-style gumbo most certainly originates. In South Carolina, you can find benne soup prepared with sesame originally brought from West Africa. *Accara*, the black-eyed pea fritters that are sold on street corners throughout West Africa, from Benin to Dakar, are one and the same as the *acarajé* found in Brazil. Additionally, the Moors from northwest Africa first brought rice to Spain, specifically Valencia, from where paella hails. Valencia's iconic seafood and rice dish has interesting similarities to *thiebou jenn*, which originated in Saint-Louis, the former French colonial capital that borders Mauritania, then part of the Moorish empire. I can't help but think of Senegal when the traditional way of eating paella is sitting around the pan, communally eating straight from the dish, savoring the crusty soccarat from the bottom, much as we do the *xooñ* in our *thiebou jenn*.

MAURITANIA

■ Podor

■ Richard Toll

Senegal River

■ Saint-Louis

■ Louga

■

SENEGAL

DAKAR
□

■ Touba

■ Thies

Saly Portudal
■
Mbour
■
Joal

■ Kaolack

Atlantic Ocean

Gambia River

■ Tambacounda

MALI

THE GAMBIA

CASAMANCE

GUINEA-BISSAU

■ Ziguinchor

■ Kedougou

GUINEA

AFRICA

├── 50 MILES ──┤

SENEGALESE FOODWAYS

Traveling through Senegal takes you through a variety of landscapes with distinct regional histories and food specialties.

NORTH

Once the capital of French Colonial West Africa, the northern city of **Saint-Louis** is located right where the Senegal River meets the Atlantic Ocean, just south of the Sahara desert. Thanks to its location, this region is particularly abundant with seafood and is the birthplace of our national dish *thiebou jenn*. The northernmost town of Senegal, **Podor**, is a semi-arid territory populated by Fulani herders, fishermen, and millet growers. The diet here is millet-based and of course fish from the river is the principal source of protein. A local specialty is the one-pot millet couscous dish made with freshwater fish, smoked fish, and peanut flour that is known as *gniri bouna*. Podor is the capital of Yela, a music style that was inspired by the sound women make when pounding grains. Yela is believed to be the ancestor of reggae music and was popularized by Podor native and superstar singer Baaba Maal. On the south bank of the Senegal River is **Richard Toll**, an old colonial town named after noted French botanist Jean Michel Claude Richard who once served as the colony's "Chief Gardener" (*toll* means "garden" in Wolof). Under his supervision, many species were introduced to Senegal, including sugarcane, which is today the region's principal crop.

WEST COAST

South from Saint-Louis stretches the gorgeous Atlantic coastline that passes through the sleepy towns of **Louga** and **Kebemer** before landing in the fast-paced, modern city of **Dakar**. Located at the westernmost coast of Africa, this vantage point has turned the city into a melting pot where cultures from all over the world have met, including the Lebanese, French, Cape Verdian, Ivorian, Vietnamese, and now a growing Chinese community that have all strongly influenced the food scene. French bakeries and broken rice, remnants of their colonial history, are popular here. Along the coast south of Dakar is the resort area of **Saly Portudal** and fishing towns such as **Mbour** and **Joal,** where artisanal fish drying, smoking, and fermenting dominate the industry. The smoke and funky smell are eased by the open air and proximity to the ocean, and the diet here is millet-based.

INLAND

Inland, about 70 kilometers from Dakar, is **Thies**, Senegal's second largest city. Thies is known as the city of railroads, since it once was a major hub that connected Senegal to Mali. Further inland is **Touba**, the holy city of Mouridism and birthplace of the popular spiced coffee drink, café Touba. Touba is located in the heart of the peanut belt and the fields are mostly tended by *talibés* (faithfuls) for the community. Every year, close to two million *talibés* assemble in Touba for a pilgrimage known as Magal Touba in commemoration of Amadou Bamba's return from exile. During the

pilgrimage, large communal cooking takes place in the vicinity of the mosques for all the visitors to eat, and rhythmic Khasaid chants (poetic prayers written by Amadou Bamba) can be heard from different mosques' loudspeakers or from live drumming and singers. South from Touba is **Kaolack**, reputed to be the hottest city in Senegal. It's the peanut-growing and salt-harvesting capital of Senegal. Kaolack can be chaotic with its urban transportation system dominated by speeding motorcycle taxis also known as "jakartas."

SOUTHWEST

Further south on the coast, after crossing the Gambia and its namesake river, is the *verdoyant* **Casamance**. The green, tropical landscape is strikingly different from the rest of Senegal and the cultural influences arguably the most diverse, including French, Portuguese (former colonizers of Guinea-Bissau in the south), Diola, Mandinka (or Socé), and Fulani. This cocktail of cultures, combined with the generous coastal land watered by abundant rainfalls and two rivers, Casamance and Gambia, has given birth to a rich and diverse cuisine. The dominant grain is rice, which has been cultivated since time immemorial. Dishes like the Portuguese-influenced *caldou*, carp fish cooked in a light lemon-based broth over rice with tomato and okra, the grilled chicken or fish *yassa* prepared with lime-onion confit, and the hearty *soupou kandja*, an okra stew with palm oil and seafood, are among the many local favorites. Here, people take their time; the pace is slow and so is the food.

SOUTHEAST

Opposite Casamance, in the eastern inland area at the foot of the Fouta Djallon mountain, lie the **Kedougou** and **Tambacounda** regions, bordering Guinea and Mali and home of the national wildlife reserve Niokolo Koba and the Dindefelo Falls. The area is mainly inhabited by Bassari and Fulani people, and fonio is the principal grain. Shea butter and palm oil are also widely produced. The temperature in the region can reach record levels of above 100°F.

TASTING SENEGAL

Those who have never tasted West African food may be pleasantly surprised by how familiar the flavors and ingredients are. When you take a bite of Senegal, here's what you'll taste.

- A blank canvas of grains such as rice, millet, *fonio*, and sorghum, on which the highly flavored main dishes shine

- The richness of meats stewed slowly on the bone, unctuous palm oil, and ground peanuts and sesame seeds

- The deep umami-rich essence of smoked, dried, and fermented fish, mollusks, and locust beans that bring the funk to the Senegalese plate

- The char and smoke of meat, whole fish, and shrimp grilled over wood charcoal and open flames

- The clean oceanic taste of freshly caught sea urchins, oysters, and clams, steamed or grilled

- Fresh vegetables and legumes, often grown in one's own garden: okra, eggplant, black-eyed peas, and the onions, tomatoes, peppers, and garlic used as a flavor base much like the sofrito of Latin American cooking, the French mirepoix, or the holy trinity of Cajun cooking

- Comforting hearty vegetables such as sweet potatoes, yuca, plantains, and pumpkin

- A slight bitterness from the dark leafy greens of sweet potatoes, sorrel, yuca, and *moringa*—easily substituted with spinach, kale, collards, Swiss chard, or mustard greens

- The brightness of lemon and lime and the fruity heat of Scotch bonnet peppers that cut through the richness

- Flavorful accents of warming ginger, tart and tangy tamarind and hibiscus, and fresh, herbaceous parsley, cilantro, and thyme

- Hints of tropical sweetness from coconuts, mangoes, bananas, and baobab

- Well-loved adopted flavors and foods from around the world: Vietnamese spring rolls, Moroccan merguez and cumin, Portuguese pastels, Lebanese kebabs, and French baguettes and strong Dijon mustard

FOOD IN DAILY LIFE

BREAKFAST

Breakfast in Senegal differs greatly between urban and rural areas. In the city, freshly baked baguettes served with spreads such as butter or chocolate and wrapped in newspaper to go are sold from kiosks on every street corner and go for about 100 CFA or 25 cents each. Pastries such as croissants— another remnant of the French—are also an increasingly popular option. The accompanying beverage of choice could be an herb tea made with *kenkelibah* leaves, instant Nescafé coffee, or much better, the uniquely Senegalese spiced café Touba (page 296) sold by ever-present street vendors.

For a hot breakfast sandwich, find yourself a *tangana*, popular eateries housed in shacks in which the cooking is done on small propane burners. A *tangana*, meaning "it's hot" in Wolof, is an indispensable morning stop for many Senegalese. Get your baguette *akk omelette*—stuffed with a fried egg, french fries, and a smear of spicy pepper sauce—and you've got yourself the perfect breakfast after dancing to *mbalax* until daybreak. Whether stuffed with beans, tuna, or even spaghetti, the sandwich is a simple affair, but it gets the job done—just don't forget to wash it down with a hot coffee sweetened with condensed milk that's quite similar to its Vietnamese counterpart.

In rural areas, mornings begin much differently. You may wake to the cadenced rhythm of the mortar and pestle (what I like to think of as our food processor) as the household's women prepare the ingredients for the coming day's meals. Healthier than city breakfasts, in the country we often eat millet porridge topped with sweet curdled milk (*lakh*) or simply sweetened with honey or sugar.

LUNCH

Every day at noon, the whole country seems to stop. Everyone comes home for lunch because in our society, this vital moment is spent together with friends and family. Lunch is prepared with great care by expert hands, and regardless of one's means, it is a matter of great pride for women to prepare a good meal. The preparation can take hours because the ingredients are usually fresh and unprocessed—slow food at its best.

All over Senegal, lunch consists of a large rice or millet dish prepared in a traditional way. Of course a perennial favorite is *thiebou jenn rouge* or *blanc*, depending on the color of the dish—*rouge* (red) for the rice cooked in a rich tomato broth and *blanc* (white) without the tomato.

TEA TIME

After lunch, family time is extended with a tea ceremony called *attaya* that may also occur throughout the day. This is the time when we connect with one another, sharing stories of our day at work, the market, or school. As I discussed in *Yolele!*, three rounds of green tea, made with fresh mint and sugar, are served in symbolic sequence, *Les Trois Normaux*: the first cup is bitter, like life; the second is sweet, like love; and the third is gentle, like the breath of death. The tea is poured slowly from high above in a long stream, back and forth, until a nice amount of foam accumulates on top.

AFTERNOON SNACK

Late afternoon, at the *takkusan* hour from about 5:00 pm to 7:00 pm when the sun starts to set and the day cools, many street corners are transformed into rustic take-out businesses selling street foods. Women install a simple setup with a wooden stool, a small table, and a wood charcoal stove (*fourneau*) on which they cook all kinds of delicious snacks: millet beignets (page 267), spicy black-eyed pea fritters called *accara* (page 101), fried plantains, crunchy roasted peanuts called *chaff*, and fried Portuguese-influenced pastries called *pastels* that might be stuffed with the sardine-like *kobo* fish and served with a spicy tomato sauce.

DINNER

After a filling midday meal, dinner is usually lighter and simpler. It may consist of fried fish with salad or french fries, or stewed meat and beans. There are, of course, the late night bites (see page 112) to look forward to.

TERANGA

As in many cultures, food in Senegal is never only to nourish the body: it's an act of sharing, of showing your love toward others, and bringing people together. If you spend time in Senegal, at some point you'll most likely hear about *teranga*, which in Wolof means "hospitality" or "welcoming generosity." The word embodies how highly the Senegalese value the act of giving, in which wealth is measured not by how much you have but by how much you give away. If Senegal could be captured in one word, it would be *teranga*—it is a value deeply embedded in the culture and thus informs a society that emphasizes the community over the individual. The attribute is a great source of pride, and even the beloved Senegalese national soccer team is known as the "Lions of Teranga." Offering *teranga* to a guest or even a stranger is most often symbolized by sharing food. We believe that when food is shared, our bowl will remain plentiful.

EATING AROUND THE BOWL

With mealtime comes the hand-washing ritual. There are different ways to do it: The simple way uses just a basin of water or a spout with running water. The more formal way uses a *satala* to pour water over a guest's hands with a calabash placed underneath to collect the washing water. (The *satala* is a kettle also used for a cleansing ritual before Muslim prayer.) After the hand-washing ritual, the family sits on the floor on a straw mat around the communal bowl to eat. Some use a spoon, but others, like myself, prefer their hand as the food tastes better this way. It may seem messy to newcomers, but for the practiced Senegalese, you won't ever see a stray drop of palm oil on a pristine white *boubou*.

Eating around the bowl with your hand is also a sign of love and trust toward those sharing the food with you. This familial practice is always an opportunity to teach certain values to children. As they're taught only to eat from the part of the bowl in front of them and not to cherry-pick around, children learn the idea of being content with what you have. Other expressions of bowl etiquette, such as finishing what's in your mouth before grabbing for more or not rushing at the food, instill a sense of patience and moderation. If you are the honored guest, you might also find that your dinner companions will stop eating before you to ensure you'll have enough.

Passersby or unexpected guests are always invited to join in and eat—without chairs, plates, and utensils, there's always room for another around the bowl. When you're finished eating, tidy up your eating area and leave the bowl to make room for anyone else who wants to eat.

》 *Rules of the Bowl for Kids*

1. Only eat the food in front of your spot; don't reach across or pick around the bowl.

2. Finish eating what's in your mouth first before putting your hand back in the bowl for more.

3. Don't rush at the food.

4. Wait for Maman to distribute the meat or vegetables (usually placed in the center of the bowl) before grabbing for it.

5. Be silent and learn to master your tongue.

6. Keep your eyes lowered to learn self-control.

7. Hold the side of the bowl with your left hand, a sign of politeness and humility.

SACRED FOOD

Every moment of life, from regular days to special occasions such as births, weddings, funerals, or religious celebrations, is centered around food. It is during these special celebrations that food takes on sacred meaning and its preparation is always a community affair.

CHILDBIRTH (NGENTÉ)

In Senegal, the *ngenté*, or naming ceremony, is a Muslim childbirth celebration traditionally held seven days after the baby is born. The baby is given its Muslim name and its head is shaved. There are gifts and, of course, lots of food. This tradition calls for a feast: those with means often slaughter a lamb for the occasion, while others may celebrate with chicken and rice pilaf (*thiebou guinaar*) or a couscous dish, and millet beignets. It is also customary to send guests home with coconut or wheat beignets wrapped in plastic bags as a form of charity that will bring blessings to the newborn. Regardless of the budget, the symbolic *lakh*, a millet porridge with sweetened curdled milk, is *de rigueur*.

INITIATION (BUKUT)

In Casamance, the *bukut* initiation rite signifies the passage from childhood to adulthood for men. The ritual happens every twenty-five to thirty years, once a generation, when hundreds, sometimes thousands, of young men gather in the sacred forest to be initiated. *Bukut* is at the core of Diola cultural identity and links the individual to the community and the community to the ancestors. The initiates are bonded for life. A person who has not been initiated is never considered an adult regardless of his age. During the initiation, they will be taught lessons on the mysteries of the universe, participating in secret rituals and physical tests. The true teaching of the initiation has an esoteric aspect and must always remain a mystery that initiates are forbidden to reveal to non-initiates. The initiation can last several days or as long as three to four months. When the men finally come out, the whole community partakes in a huge celebration with drums, dancing, and food. Several bulls are slaughtered and the festivities can go on for several days. The family members of the newly initiated prepare a feast that's brought to the celebration in large communal bowls. The bowls, full of a wide variety of dishes, are shared in a giant potluck. Groups organically assemble around different bowls depending on one's food preference.

MARRIAGE (TAKK)

A marriage celebration can take different forms in Senegal, but it is always an occasion of great festivities. The party begins after the religious ritual that usually takes place at the mosque or church, depending on the couple's religious affiliation. Traditionally, symbolic cola nuts are given as an offering to bless the couple. The banquet dinner is served family-style with large platters of food placed on straw mats that people sit around in groups to eat. Whereas DJs are often hired to play music in the cities, in rural areas such as Casamance, weddings are celebrated with live drumming, sometimes accompanied by a saxophonist who walks alongside the newlyweds in a dancing procession to the party locale.

DEATH (DEE)

At my dad's funeral, because of his elderly status, my siblings and I were required to offer a bull for the celebration. My uncles, cousins, and some friends slaughtered and skinned the bull in the backyard. It was immediately butchered and sent to the women in a makeshift kitchen, an open area outside where big logs of wood were fueling giant cast-iron pots. This kitchen was the center of activities for the weeklong funeral, and the women were expected to feed hundreds of people every day. It is common that many people show up at a funeral; not all of them particularly knew the deceased, but such an occasion is always an opportunity for free food. The act of sharing food with the wayfarer is considered an offering, a *sarakh*, beneficial to both the living and the dead.

Other relatives brought contributions to my dad's passing feast: a whole pig (for the non-Muslims), countless chickens, and guinea hens. The women organized themselves in brigades, some plucking fowl, others pounding grains with giant mortars and pestles.

Every day at noon that week, large bowls and platters full of victuals such as *thiebou yapp* (rice and beef pilaf), chicken *yassa*, and roasted ducks and guinea hens were taken from the kitchen to the courtyard where the crowd gathered. Small groups sat around each platter, and after washing their hands, proceeded to eat. The atmosphere was no longer sad, but convivial.

RELIGIOUS FOODS

About 95 percent of Senegalese people are Muslim, the vast majority of which belong to the Sufi tradition of Islamic mysticism, while the remaining 5 percent practice Christianity. Many Senegalese, regardless of religious belief, take part in traditional customs, and all are bound by a strong sense of community values including *teranga* (hospitality), *kersa* (respect for others), and *tegin* (good manners). A beautiful tradition of peace and tolerance can be observed in Senegal during the religious holidays in which Muslims and Christians offer generous portions of festive food to each other and the needy.

Tabaski (*Eid al-Adha* or Feast of the Sacrifice) is a Muslim holiday to commemorate Abraham's sacrifice of a ram instead of his son. For the occasion, arguably the biggest holiday in Senegal, every Senegalese Muslim household slaughters a lamb or a ram, depending on one's means. Nothing is wasted, and the whole animal is used for the feast. Everything—the head, the liver, kidneys, tripe, and testicles—is prepared in a special way for the enjoyment of all, and it's an excellent opportunity for chefs to show off their cooking skills. For this holiday in particular, it is customary to divide the meat into portions to deliver to the needy and to Christian friends and neighbors—no one is forgotten.

A few weeks following *Tabaski* comes *Tamkharit*, which marks the Muslim New Year. In Senegal, it's always a carnival-like celebration as children dress up and go around the neighborhood singing and dancing in return for sugar, candy, rice, or a few coins. It's our Senegalese Halloween. The traditional *Tamkharit* meal is *thiéré bassi*, an elaborate, delicious dish of rich lamb stew with *moringa* or baobab greens served over a fine millet couscous with dates and white beans. Once most of the meat and vegetables are eaten, we pour milk over the couscous and finish it off for an extra special treat. You must eat the *thiéré bassi* until you're stuffed to ensure that you'll be full for all of the next year. Afterward, one by one, you drop your bowl or plate onto the floor to make a wish or receive blessings for the new year.

On the Christian calendar, for Good Friday Senegalese traditionally prepare *ngalakh*, a creamy, sweet, and tangy millet couscous dish made with baobab fruit and peanut butter, and share it with Muslim neighbors. Later in the year, Christmas in Dakar is always a family affair. On Christmas Eve, we usually have a big potluck in which my mother and aunts cook their Senegalese version of a typical Christmas dinner: roast turkey with onion-rich *yassa* sauce, rice pilaf, green beans, and sometimes even a yule log cake for dessert. On Christmas Day, we always have a lunch for all our friends and neighbors.

AFROEATS

Sadly, during colonial times a myth was fabricated, claiming that the native crops of Africa were not as nutritious as the imported ones. This situation facilitated the introduction of new cash crops needed for European markets and the displacement of native crops that came to be seen as second-rate. Throughout the colonized continent, farmers were encouraged to produce cash crops such as tea, coffee, cocoa, peanuts, or cotton while subsistence foods such as rice, wheat, and maize were imported.

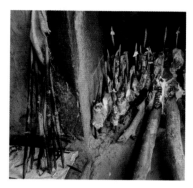

As a result, traditional food crops such as millet, *fonio*, and Diola rice are now seen as peasant food. Meanwhile, in the cities, mornings begin with the classic European breakfast of *pain-beurre,* a baguette baked with imported wheat flour and served with butter likewise imported from Normandy, France.

For lunch, although Senegalese people still prefer traditional dishes, the rice that often serves as their base is imported from Southeast Asia rather than the domestic rice grown in the south in Casamance or in the northern fields of the Senegal River Valley. A majority of the national consumption of rice is imported, crushing the local competition.

My friend, Mieko Ikegame, who is the Former Director of the United Nations Office of the Special Adviser on Africa and has worked extensively in mobilizing international support for the peace and development of the continent, told me, "On the basis of my experience in the United Nations for the last 30 years, it is my strong conviction that Africa will be the leading region of the world in many decades to come. Needless to say, the promotion and recognition of African food and agricultural production are essential to the food security and sustainable development of the continent. Moreover, they are critical not only for Africa, but for the rest of the world. According to the Food and Agriculture Organization of the United Nations, what mankind at the global level requires to feed itself for the next 40 years is the amount of food produced in the past 4,000 years. Most importantly, 60% of arable land on this earth is on the African continent."

With the demand around the world for healthy ingredients growing, the food of Africa is poised to play a major role once again. Nutritionists are recognizing ingredients like *fonio*, millet, palm oil, and many others of African origin for their enormous nutritional wealth. These products, once considered second-rate, are beginning to be enjoyed by those outside of rural populations.

Supermarkets specializing in selling local products are increasingly gaining popularity among locals. Among the pioneers of this locavore movement is Mme. Aissatou Diagne Deme with her supermarket, Supermarché 100% Afrique. Aware of the opportunities arising from this shift, other Senegalese entrepreneurs, mostly women engaged in local food production, have been striving to transform the movement into something more permanent than just a fleeting trend.

THE BIRTH OF AFROEATS

It was in this spirit that we decided to launch AfroEats, the first festival of its kind dedicated to the promotion of local food and food products of Africa. Teaming with designers Bibi Seck and Fati Ly, we started discussing the concept and how it could have the biggest impact. *"Lekk sunuy mégnéf"* ("Let's eat what we produce") became the rallying cry for the AfroEats movement. We were soon joined by Fatou Mboup, a dynamic event planner based in Dakar who brought along a network of women's organizations involved with local food production and the famed ITA (the visionary Institute of Food Technology based in Dakar). The turning point came when we met Ibrahima Basse, the director of industry at the Senegalese Department of Commerce. Mr. Basse immediately understood the scope of our vision and facilitated access to government contacts and resources that would bring it to reality.

From May 1 to May 5, 2013, in the gardens of the giant Chinese-built Grand National Theater in downtown Dakar, AfroEats was launched. Close to a hundred exhibitors, all locals, showcased their products. Students from cooking schools participated in a competition using only local ingredients, in which the best dish would be crowned winner. Inside the theater, seminars and workshops were led by chefs, nutritionists, and food scholars from Senegal and around the world. Workshops included Nutrition and Technology, Traditional Flavor Enhancers versus the Dangers of "Cubism" (abuse of bouillon cubes), African Gastronomy and the World, African Restaurants and Culinary Tourism, and so forth.

As part of the festival, I brought along a culinary delegation from the United States. Among the diverse group of participating chefs were Anita Lo of Annisa, Abdoul Gueye of Abistro, Samuel Beket of Hill Café, Dave Arnold of Booker and Dax and founder of the New York Museum of Food, Alexander Smalls of The Cecil and Minton's, and chef Eric Simeon of CitiGroup. Joining the group from Paris was pastry chef Mickaël Azouz and the popular Cameroonian chef and TV personality Christian Abegan.

Among the scholars was Jessica Harris, cookbook author and doyenne of African American culinary history. Jessica hadn't been in Senegal for over twenty years, so it was a true pleasure to see her reconnect with a country of which she is so fond. I was particularly proud to be with her, as she has always been an inspiration to me—and as it turned out, she was also acquainted with my family friends in Senegal. Another good friend who joined the delegation was Mexican scholar Marco Polo Hernández Cuevas. Marco has written extensively about the African influence in Mexican cuisine and his participation was indispensable.

In addition to participating in the seminars, the group went on a culinary tour designed to introduce the sources of Senegalese cuisine. One evening was spent with chef Mawa Hugues who taught the basics of the Senegalese pantry and cooked us a feast of Senegalese classics, from *mbakhalou saloum* (rice and black-eyed peas with dried mullet, smoked sardinelles, and fermented conch), *gourmbane* (steamed millet with beef and peanut stew), *thiebou jenn* (page 204), *thiebou yapp* (a one-pot rice and meat dish reminiscent of jambalaya), *mafé*, and *thiéré mboum* (*moringa* and millet couscous stew).

One very early morning was spent on a fishing trip with my friend Ousmane (see page 194), a local Lébou fisherman who lives in the village of Ouakam. Riding out in beautifully painted wooden boats, we watched as Ousmane did his work, quickly filling the hull with shimmering silver fish.

Of course we ate and ate. A favorite spot was La Pointe, a collection of fish stands along the coast just a walk down the road from the chefs' hotel. Sitting at makeshift tables and watching the sun go down on the Atlantic, the spectacular views were matched only by the incredible fresh seafood at our disposal. There was seafood of all kinds, all caught that very day: sea urchins, clams, lobsters, shrimp, barnacles, and *thioff*, Senegal's local iconic fish, all simply steamed or grilled. The chefs were particularly excited by the barnacles, prized in Spain where they fetch a pretty penny. Eaten with bare hands and washed down with a cold Gazelle beer, meals here were many and memorable.

As there is no better way to get immersed in Senegalese society than to visit the markets, we spent time at the colorful and crowded markets of Kermel, Tilene, and HLM, where the average Senegalese go for their daily shopping. Right behind the Kermel market, we ate a lunch of *thiebou jenn* at a makeshift eatery, sitting on wooden benches alongside locals at a long communal table under a plastic tarp shielding us from the bright midday sun.

The trip brought us to Keur Moussa (see page 268), a Benedictine monastery an hour outside of Dakar that's self-sustained by its farm and orchards, and onward to the Pink Lake (see page 222) where we watched salt destined for local markets extracted from its namesake-colored waters. Last but not least, we visited Gorée Island, also known as Memory Island, a symbol of the Atlantic slave trade that brought kidnapped Africans to the Americas. After crossing the Door of No Return, wherever they landed in the New World, these Africans brought changes to local flavors and created a new Creole cuisine, unmistakably African.

On the last evening of our trip, the chefs threw a banquet for AfroEats using only local ingredients. It was fascinating to see how just a few days of immersion into our cuisine had sparked such creativity among the participating chefs. We wowed the diners with Chef Abegan's smoky and light *ndolé* made with shrimp and cassava leaves, Chef Abdoul's rice croquettes with mango coulis, Chef Marco's Senegalese-inspired ceviche, Dave Arnold's famous *madd* and rum cocktail, and my own *fonio* and mint salad with lime vinaigrette, to name a few. That night, when it all ended, I had a feeling of having achieved the ultimate *teranga*.

AfroEats was the first of its kind and a welcome contribution to the growing chorus of voices that want to reverse the trend of food imports into Africa and highlight our local products. The festival's greatest achievement is that it had assembled scholars, politicians, entrepreneurs, and chefs under the same roof for a necessary conversation. Once all these actors begin to consciously collaborate, the impact will be greater than the sum of its parts.

HOW TO USE THIS BOOK

This book is meant to transport you deep into the vibrant, diverse food scene of Senegal. You'll feel the sun at your back coupled with the cool breeze off the Atlantic, hear the sound of freshly caught *thioff* hitting the grill, and maybe even catch a whiff of a little fermented fish funk in the air.

Some of the recipes are traditional classics of Senegalese cooking, while most are my own creative takes inspired by those traditions. No recipe is ever set in stone. I hope that readers will be inspired by the recipes, the stories, and Evan Sung's beautiful photography, feeling free to experiment with their own local and loved ingredients. Senegalese cooking does not require a heap of ingredients you don't already have, but there will be a few special ones you'll want to seek out. Don't worry, it'll be easy to do with our list of sources (see page 314). Hopefully as West African food becomes more popular, it'll be even easier.

Feel free to mix and match recipes to create your own Senegalese feast. Maybe you'll start with a big fresh salad and dive into a spread of the many street foods and snacks we Senegalese love to eat. There are of course many main dishes to tuck into that are essentially one-pot meals where the savory meat, vegetables, and grain richly fold into one. Other stews may require just a simple side of rice, millet, or *fonio* to sop up all that good gravy (a heel of French bread to assist never hurts, either). Grilled meats and fish are pure and simple in preparation, but hit next-level status with the addictive punch of an herbaceous sauce or a spicy salsa. Some recipes will require some slow and low cooking, but that too is in the spirit of Senegal—take your time and enjoy it. As with any cookbook, be sure to read the entire recipe before you start cooking as some recipes require overnight marinating time.

More than just a collection of recipes, this book is about where our food comes from and why you should care. Throughout, you'll learn about the different regions of Senegal and their unique cooking styles and ingredients. We'll have conversations with Senegal's food producers, chefs, and other cultural figures to get a deeper understanding of food's place in Senegalese society. There will be the occasional guest recipe from some of my chef colleagues and friends who have been inspired by their experiences in Senegal. You won't just be learning to make a few dishes; you'll learn about the Senegalese people, the stories of our past, and importantly, the issues we face today and will confront tomorrow.

THE SENEGALESE KITCHEN

Luckily, Senegalese cooking does not require a whole slew of new ingredients you have to search to the end of the earth for. These are basic ingredients to stock up on, some of which you may already have now. Most will be easy to find or have simple substitutions, but there are of course a few that are worth seeking out in the spirit of trying something new and distinctly Senegalese.

GRAINS

No Senegalese meal feels complete without a grain, most often rice, to soak up all the delicious, deeply flavored gravy. Although many Senegalese, particularly those living in urban areas, have come to favor broken rice over more traditional (and nutritious) whole grains, I hope that tide will change.

FINGER MILLET

Known as *dugub* in Senegal, finger millet is a major staple grain in Africa and South Asia. It was one of the first crops to be domesticated in Africa thousands of years ago, and today, Africa produces about 2 million tons of millet of the world's annual production of 4.5 million. It is highly nutritious, hardy, and drought resistant, but despite its many values, production has greatly decreased in the last decades, and it has been largely ignored by the scientific community. However, it has come into the spotlight in the West due in some degree to the increased interest in alternative gluten-free grains. Compared to pearl millet, which is the more common variety you'll find, finger millet has a darker complexion and earthier taste.

Finger millet is traditionally processed by women with a mortar and pestle. It has a nutty aroma and is most often steamed and served alongside main dishes as rice or couscous would be, or ground into flour to be used in bread baking. Millet couscous (*araw*) is made from millet that has been ground into flour and then shaped into couscous of varying sizes. It is then steamed, dried, and packaged. The very fine grains, *thiéré*, and the small broken grains, *sankhal*, are used in the moringa stew *sauce mboum*, the porridge-like *bassi salté*, or as a side to meat, fish, or vegetables. Medium grains, *thiakry*, can also be eaten as a side or used in *ngalakh* porridge. Finally, the largest grains are used for the sweet porridge known as *fondé*. Finger millet can be found in African markets or through online retailers. Semolina couscous or hulled millet can be used as a substitute for the fine- to medium-sized millet couscous.

FONIO

One of the most nutritious grains you can find, *fonio* is a very small seed-like type of millet that is also one of Africa's oldest grains, cultivated in West Africa for thousands of years. *Fonio* is rich in important amino acids (cystine and methionine), high in fiber, gluten-free, and has a low glycemic index. It is one of the fastest-maturing grains, highly adaptable in difficult growing conditions, resistant to drought, and able to thrive in poor soil. In Senegal, it is grown in the southeast in Tambacounda and Kedougou and in the south in Casamance.

    Fonio is fluffy and a little nutty when steamed or cooked pilaf-style, comparable to couscous or quinoa. It can be used as a nutritious substitute for rice and couscous, made into a light grain salad, cooked down to porridge, or even ground into flour for baking. The Senegalese often prepare it with baobab leaves or ground okra. As of now, it is available in West African shops and from online importers, but my hope is to make it more widely known and available to the general public. If you can't find it, quinoa, couscous, or millet would make a good substitute.

RICE

Rice is a huge part of the Senegalese diet. *Oryza glaberrima* is one of two principal varieties of rice native to West Africa. Commonly referred to as "red rice" for its reddish outer bran, it is cultivated in the Casamance region, and is different from Bhutanese or Camargue red rice. Red rice is considered prestigious and is also used for special occasions and rituals. Broken rice (see page 182), the smaller pieces of rice leftover from processing and imported cheaply from Asia, is especially common and preferred in urban areas. Once cooked, it has a softer texture than regular rice and is often used in *thiebou jenn*. You can find broken rice in West African, Thai, and Vietnamese shops or through online retailers. You can also make your own by briefly pulsing jasmine rice in a food processor.

SORGHUM

Sorghum is another nutritious staple whole grain of Africa that is drought resistant and very hardy. It is high in fiber, iron, protein, and antioxidants, and since it's gluten-free, it has recently come into the spotlight in the West. Milled to a fine powder, it is now commonly found in gluten-free flour blends. In Africa, you can find it used just like rice in stews or one-pot dishes, but most commonly in stiff porridges called *sadza* in Zimbabwe, *ugali* in Tanzania, or *bogobe* in Nigeria. It is also brewed for a beer called *dolo* in Burkina Faso. Sorghum has an earthy taste and in Senegal is often served slightly fermented with a tomato, onion, and okra broth. In rural Senegal, it is first pounded into flour before hand-processed into couscous. You can find whole sorghum grains in West African markets, Indian markets, or in natural foods stores.

ESSENTIALS

HIBISCUS (BISAAP)

Dried red and white hibiscus petals, specifically *Hibiscus sabdariffa*, bring a bright, tart, cranberry-like flavor to many drinks and dishes in Senegal. Throughout West Africa, it's referred to as *bisaap*, but you may be familiar with its other names, especially when it comes in its popular tea form: roselle, sorrel in the Caribbean, or *agua de jamaica* throughout Latin America. *Bisaap blanc*, the white flowers, will be a bit milder than the red variety. You can find dried hibiscus at African, Latin American, or Middle Eastern groceries and through online retailers. Depending on the source, you may have to rinse them under cold water to clean them before use. The leaves of the hibiscus, commonly called sorrel, are also used. Sorrel has a slightly acidic flavor and is often made into *baguedj*, a condiment combined with okra and served with the fish dish, *caldou*. The leaves may also be eaten raw in a salad. Look for sorrel leaves at gourmet stores and farmers' markets in the spring.

PEANUT PRODUCTS

In the 1970s and '80s, Senegal ranked among the largest peanut producers in the world. Peanuts first arrived in West Africa from South America through the Columbian Exchange and were quickly embraced as a valuable and sustainable food source. Before the arrival of peanuts, groundnuts, a similar legume from the same family, were very popular in West Africa. Also known as the Bambara pea after the ethnic group from Mali, groundnuts were quickly usurped by peanuts and are now cultivated only in the southeastern part of Senegal. Through the slave trade, peanuts made their way back to North America and became a major cash crop in the southern United States.

The Senegalese love peanuts in lots of different ways. You'll see them everywhere as a snack in Senegal: boiled in salt water (*mbakhal*, page 118), roasted in hot sand (*gerté chaff*), or crystallized in sugar (*gerté sukar,* page 119). Pounded into peanut butter, they're used as a base for the rich popular dish *mafé* (page 242). If using commercial peanut butter in the recipes, make sure it is natural, smooth, and unsweetened.

Ground into flour, they're used in the traditional Kan Kan Kan Spice Mix (page 87) and as a thickener in stews such as *sauce feuille*. You can find packaged peanut flour in West African groceries and health-food stores, but making it yourself is very easy. If you only need a little bit of peanut flour, simply grind a few tablespoons of skinned, raw peanuts in a coffee or spice grinder. Larger amounts can be pulsed in a food processor, but be very careful not to overprocess or you will get peanut butter, not the fine flour you want.

RED PALM FRUIT OIL (DIWTIIR)

Red palm oil, pressed from palm fruit, is essential to Senegalese cooking. The unrefined virgin red palm fruit oil is the type to seek out—not the colorless palm kernel oil, pressed from the kernels rather than the fruit. Popular in Brazil, it may be found by its Portuguese name, *dende*. Virgin red palm oil is very different from the highly processed palm oil that is found in many processed snack foods stocked in your grocery aisles.

Palm oil, rich and dark, has a slightly savory intensity that enhances the flavors of other foods it's cooked with. There really is no substitute for it and I urge you to seek it out especially now that it's easier to find than ever. Look in your local Whole Foods Market, health-food stores, gourmet food shops, and Brazilian and West African groceries, or through online retailers. If you absolutely can't find it, vegetable oil or butter will suffice in the recipes.

SELIM PEPPER (DJAR)

Senegalese cooking does not use very many spices, but one exception is the uniquely West African pepper: *selim*. *Selim* pepper may go by many other names including *djar*, grains of Selim, *selim kili*, *kimba* pepper, African pepper, Senegal pepper, and Guinea pepper (not to be confused with the other peppers that go by that same name). Consisting of dark brown pods that contain black shiny seeds, *selim* pepper is highly aromatic and spicy, with a hint of nutmeg and bitterness. It is often smoked in its preparation, which further intensifies its deep musk. It can be added whole or crushed to gamy, meaty stews or ground into a rub for fish or meat. Most often, though, you'll find it ground in the iconic Senegalese coffee drink, café Touba. *Selim* pepper is essential to café Touba, giving it an intense peppery kick. When used ground, crack open the pods and remove the seeds, which can be bitter; toast the pods and grind in a spice grinder. Look for *selim* pepper in any specialty spice shop.

》》 *A Note About the Palm Oil Controversy*

Recently, tropical oils such as palm oil and especially coconut oil have experienced a surge in popularity due to their lauded health benefits—full of vitamins A and E, antioxidants, and co-enzyme Q10. These oils have long been thought of as "bad for you" due to their levels of saturated fat, which has been linked to LDL ("bad") cholesterol and heart disease. However, some recent studies suggest that saturated fat should not be demonized as it once was, and perhaps that link is not so clear. In addition, there's a lot to be said about where that fat comes from: whether it's plant-based or animal-based, processed or unprocessed, red meat or dairy, could make a difference.

Another issue that you may hear about is the environmental impact of palm oil production, specifically relating to deforestation and orangutan habitats in Southeast Asia, where most of the world's palm oil comes from. For your own cooking, make sure to look for the rich, red West African palm oil or others that specifically note their origins. In 2004, the Roundtable of Sustainable Palm Oil was formed to address such issues. As with all such matters, health-related or ecological, my best advice is to do your research and make an informed decision for yourself.

BRING IN THE FUNK: SMOKED, FERMENTED, AND DRIED FLAVOR AGENTS

The Senegalese use a variety of dried, fermented, and smoked fish and mollusks in small amounts to add a deep, umami essence to many soups, stews, and sauces. These products form the backbone of our cuisine. Like the use of anchovies, dried bonito flakes, ham hocks, and bacon in other cultures, the fish contributes a strong, rich, savory flavor that keeps you coming back for more. *Guedj*, which has a strong pungent smell, is made from white-fleshed fish such as sea bream, catfish, croaker, and skate, and sometimes larger fish such as rays, sharks, and large mackerel. There's also *tambadiang*, made from bonito, and *kethiakh*, made from small sardine-like fish that's charred then smoked and dried in ovens, *banda*-style. Mollusks get similar treatments: there are *yeet* and *toufa*, conch-like sea snails fermented and dried in sand, *yokhoss* (smoked oysters), and *paañ* (sun-dried clams).

It is estimated that 70 percent of all fish sold and marketed in Africa is cured. However, in areas such as Senegal, where there is very good access to fresh fish, those proportions are reversed; in Senegal, only about 15 percent is consumed cured. The preferred curing methods, often in combination, include hot-smoking over trenches or in mud-walled kilns, salting, sun-drying, and fermenting in sacks buried in the ground. To hot smoke the traditional way, the fish is placed over unlined trenches in the earth filled with a smoldering fire of wood and grass. The fish is then covered with grass mats and left to smoke for several days. The processing is traditionally dominated by women, though men are involved in the marketing.

All these funky friends can be found in African groceries or online, but as a substitute, use a high-quality Vietnamese or Thai fish sauce as many Senegalese do out of convenience. Chinese markets also have dried fish products such as dried oysters and shrimp that could bring in the funk, so to speak. Sadly, there is also a growing trend of using artificial, MSG-laden seasonings such as Maggi or Jumbo to achieve that depth of flavor, but none stand close to the real thing.

Nététou, also called *dawadawa* or *soumbala*, is neither fish nor mollusk, but belongs in this category for its equally pungent purpose in the kitchen. Made from fermented, dried African locust beans, *nététou* is similar to and can be substituted with Chinese fermented black beans.

Kong

Moringa

White Hibiscus

Red Hibiscus

Baobab

Guedj

Okra

Yeet

Sorrel

Red Palm Oil

Broken Rice

Cowpeas

Broken Millet

Black-eyed Peas

Guedj

Yokhoss

Nététou

Toufa

Dried Shrimp

Paañ

Yuca

Butternut Squash

Guedj

Tamarind

Calabash

Kethiakh

Bitter Eggplant

Tomatoes

Scotch Bonnet

Limes

LE POTAGER DU SENEGAL

These are some of my favorite Senegalese vegetables that find their way from backyard gardens to the stewpot.

BITTER EGGPLANT (JAXATU)

Bitter eggplant, also known as *jaxatu*, are usually picked before maturity and resemble a yellow or green tomato, sometimes with vertical striping. They have an intense, bitter flavor and are often used in sauces and stews. In addition to the fruit, the leaves are also boiled and used as a side dish. If you're lucky, you can find them frozen in West African groceries.

COWPEAS/BLACK-EYED PEAS

Cowpeas were one of the many ingredients African slaves brought with them to the Americas. If cowpeas don't sound familiar, you may have heard of the very popular variety of cowpea and staple in Southern kitchens: black-eyed peas. Black-eyed peas are just one type of cowpea; heirloom varieties of cowpeas include deep red–purple peas from Burkina Faso, the Holstein pea (mottled black and white, like the cow), cream-colored peas with pink eyes, and gray-speckled peas, just to name a few. Protein-rich cowpeas remain very popular in West Africa where we use them dried or fresh from the pod in a variety of soups, salads, and stews or mashed and fried into the favorite street food *accara* (page 101). We also love using the leafy greens of the plants, especially in soups.

MORINGA

Moringa is so highly nutritious that the tree's nicknames are "miracle tree" and *nevedaye*, as in "never die." Indeed, *moringa*, whose tiny leaves taste like spinach, is jam-packed with vitamins A and C, protein, calcium, fiber, beta-carotene, and iron. The leaves can be eaten raw, sautéed, or cooked in any number of stews, soups, and dishes such as *mboum*, a traditional millet couscous stew with *moringa*, beef, and peanuts. I also love to include *moringa* in my veggie burger (page 135) or in croquette recipes. *Moringa* can come dried and ground into a powder, in which case it can be simply sprinkled over a dish or stirred into stews and soups. All parts of the plant—the bark, flowers, roots, seeds—are used for medicinal purposes. *Moringa* can be found in West African groceries, health-food stores, and through online retailers. It may be substituted with spinach or other dark leafy greens.

OKRA

Okra, one of my favorite vegetables, is very popular in Senegal and plays a symbolic role in the cuisine of southern Senegal in particular. It's used in a variety of ways: cooked whole or chopped in sauces and stews, grilled in a vegetable platter or a salad, or dried and ground to be used as a thickener for sauces. As one of the vegetables introduced to the Americas via the slave trade, okra is now a favorite in many Southern kitchens.

YUCA

The "African potato" in reality is not so African. Just like peanuts, tomatoes, and peppers, yuca arrived on our shores from the Americas during the Columbian Exchange. What's fascinating is how we embraced it and made it our own well-loved ingredient. Indeed, across West Africa, from Mali to Nigeria to Côte d'Ivoire, this hearty root vegetable enlivens the daily bowl in so many ways. When its dense, creamy-white flesh is pounded into a dough, it becomes *fufu*, the staple starch that graces many West African tables, ready to be pinched and used to scoop soups and stews. When boiled then fried, yuca makes fries (page 212) that are so crispy and moist that I'd take them over french fries any day. Whether thinly sliced and fried into chips, simply roasted, or thrown into a soup or stew, yuca is popular around the world, especially in Latin America. Other names for yuca include cassava, manioc, and tapioca (of the American favorite, tapioca pudding).

NATURALLY SWEET SENEGAL

Senegal grows a great diversity of fruits, and I always look forward to savoring them whenever I travel home. Each has a special place in my childhood memories. The ones I list here are a few of my favorite fruits that bring me right back to Senegal. Other fruits such as mango, banana, and coconut are beloved and feature prominently in Senegalese cooking as well, but I want to introduce you to some you may not have heard of before. Though it may be difficult to try them fresh here in the States, I encourage you to seek them out in whatever alternative form possible—juice, syrups, jams—through online sources or West African groceries to get a sweet taste of Senegal.

BAOBAB

Known to many Africans as the "tree of life," the baobab is considered Senegal's national tree. Baobabs are an essential part of the African savanna landscape, dominating with trunks that can grow to 50 feet in circumference and sprawling branches that look like roots spreading into the sky. (The baobab is sometimes known as the "upside down tree.")

The gourd-like fruit that hangs from its branches has a hard, fuzzy green shell and inside, a white, chalky fruit pulp known for its "superfruit" qualities. According to studies published in the journal *Critical Reviews in Food Science and Nutrition*, baobab fruit has six times the vitamin C of oranges and very high amounts of calcium and antioxidants. It's been used for centuries in Africa for its medicinal qualities and is now available in the West in supplement form. Pleasantly sweet and acidic, the pulp can be stirred into water or milk to create refreshing and nutritious drinks called *bouye*. The Fulani people combine the fruit with milk to make *sow*, a yogurt-like treat that is sweetened and served over millet porridge—one of my favorite after-school snacks growing up.

As every part of the tree is used, it is truly a life-sustaining plant. Even more commonly used than the fruit are the baobab leaves, which are rich in calcium and similar to spinach when fresh. They can be incorporated into soups, stews, and millet and make a delicious sauce called *sauce-feuilles*. The baobab kernels can be fermented and used as seasoning or eaten raw or roasted, in which case they taste like almonds. Beyond food, the baobab's bark fibers can be woven into mats, baskets, and rain hats, and the roots can be used to make a red dye.

In the West, you'll most likely find baobab as a powder that you can easily turn into smoothies and jams, sprinkle over cereal and yogurt, and incorporate into your favorite baked goods.

CASHEW FRUIT

Also known as "cashew apples," the juicy cashew fruit (technically an accessory fruit) ripens to a bright red or yellow and has a sweet, tropical flavor with strong tannic notes. The cashew nut (the plant's seed) that we love to snack on in the West grows within a poisonous shell on the outside of the fruit. Hanging from the branches, the fruits almost look like upside-down bell peppers. Native to Brazil, cashew fruits grow in tropical climates, and Nigeria is now one of the world's largest producers. Cooked with sugar, cashew fruit makes a delicious jam, and is also used to make the famous alcoholic drink *cana* in Casamance (see page 307). The fruit is also very popular in South America and India. The fruit is soft and its skin delicate, making it hard to transport. Instead, seek out the juice or fruit concentrate in bottled form.

DESERT DATES

These yellow bitter dates are called *soump* in Wolof. Grown year-round from trees found all over Senegal, they can be eaten fresh or dried. The seeds contain an oil that is rich in protein and has a delicate taste. When dried, the fruits can be used for preparing sauces or soups. The leaves are used after a long boil to remove their bitter taste.

DITAKH

Ditakh (*Detarium senegalense*) grows in the regions of Casamance and Saloum, and has an exceptionally high amount of vitamin C. The sweet fruits are small, round, and green, protected by a dull brown shell. Within, you'll find tufts of green, fibrous, strand-like pulp, which can be eaten straight from the shell. More easily found is *ditakh* juice, which is made from soaking the fruit in water, or bottled *ditakh* syrup concentrate. Like other Senegalese fruits and vegetables, many parts of the *ditakh* plant are used for medicinal purposes. Please note, there are two types of *ditakh* trees: the edible *ditakh* tree is small and has white flowers, while the other, which is much taller and grows small red berries, produces poisonous fruit and should be avoided.

MADD

The *madd* fruit may look a bit bumpy and beat-up on the outside, but cut off the top and within you'll find pitted lobes of bright yellow-orange fruit that is intensely sweet and sour. Senegalese love *madd* just sprinkled with a little sugar, salt, or hot pepper, or as a refreshing juice diluted with water or mixed with other fruit juices. Outside of Senegal, you can find it bottled as a juice or preserves; the most popular packaged brand is Zena, a Lebanese family–owned company.

TAMARIND

Tamarind, with its sticky sweet tang, is a favorite ingredient in Senegal. Tamarind's flavor can be compared to a sour date, and it is used in a wide range of dishes from millet couscous, soups, sauces, chutneys, drinks, and sweets. The tamarind tree is indigenous to Africa and was later brought by colonists and traders to Central America and South Asia, where its fruit became a well-loved, staple ingredient. Tamarind can be eaten as a snack fresh out of its pod, but you're likely to find the fruit as blocks of pulp or bottled as a concentrate or paste. If you use the pulp, you can remove the fibers and seeds by soaking it in hot water and pushing it through a fine-mesh sieve. You'll find tamarind in Asian, Latin, and West African groceries.

THE MORTAR AND PESTLE

Everywhere in Africa, the thumping sound of the mortar and pestle is the sign that the cooking has begun. Preparing a traditional lunch can take hours, and mornings in rural Senegal mean waking up to the cadenced rhythms of the huge wooden mortar and pestle, usually carved from the wood of a mango tree. If there was one instrument that symbolizes the African kitchen, it would be, without a doubt, the mortar and pestle. One of the most common images of daily African life is a woman pounding food in a wooden mortar. It's our blender, food processor, and spice grinder all in one.

Some of my most vivid memories of Senegal are of that thumping beat. At special celebrations, the air fills with the sound of women singing as they pound to the rhythm, making music and food both. Often the pounding is cadenced to accompany a song. The songs can vary depending on the occasion: funerals, weddings, births, or just a lullaby for the rocking baby, securely wrapped on the back of the woman who is pounding.

As diverse as the cuisines of all of Africa are, this heavy wooden bowl on its pedestal is the quintessential kitchen tool of the whole continent. No matter what's on the menu—whether you're pounding whole millet or herbs in Senegal, yam and green plantains for *fufu* in Nigeria or *foutou* in Côte d'Ivoire, or maize for fermented Ghanaian *kenkey* or South African *pap*—the mortar and pestle is the instrument of choice.

The mortar and pestle is more than just a kitchen appliance, as it is considered sacred in many African countries. In the West African tradition, the mortar represents the strength of the family. It is said that the head of the family should never meet someone bringing or taking a mortar from the house. In the Bambara tradition, a young newlywed bride has to sit on the mortar four times in a row. It is believed that the bride subjected to this rite would never get divorced. The bride herself always brings a symbolic mortar and pestle among her belongings when moving in with her new husband. For the Soninke people of southern Senegal, when a stranger enters a house and sees a mortar upside down with the pestle sitting at its base, it means that there was a death in the family. For that matter, the sound of the mortar should never be heard at night unless there is a funeral. The mortar is then used to crush incense for the ultimate bath of the deceased.

Mortars and pestles come in all sizes. The smallest are used to blend pepper mixtures or other spices, and the large ones, with a mortar the size of a small toddler and the pestle akin to a long baseball bat, are used to prepare millet or rice flour or to remove the hulls from grains or beans. The modern kitchen has replaced this essential tool with the electric food processor, but purists know that nothing can fully duplicate the taste and texture of food that comes from pounding by hand. Unlike the sharp blade of the modern food processor that bruises the ingredients, the pestle crushes them in a way that helps release their fresh flavors and oils, and the difference in taste is palpable. Traditionalists in some rural areas still refuse to take their whole grains to the mill—although it's faster and easier, it just doesn't taste the same.

SNACKS AND STREET FOODS

SPICE-CRUSTED PASTELS

with SMOKED MACKEREL & PICKLED MANGO

MAKES ABOUT 32 PASTELS

DOUGH

2 cups chicken stock, vegetable stock, or water

2 cups all-purpose flour, plus more for rolling

1½ teaspoons salt

FILLING

1 tablespoon vegetable or olive oil

½ yellow onion, finely chopped

2 garlic cloves, finely chopped

2 cups flaked, skinned, smoked mackerel fillet

1 tablespoon finely chopped fresh cilantro

⅔ cup Pickled Mango (recipe follows; optional)

SPICE CRUST

2 large eggs

¼ cup water

¼ cup cayenne pepper

¼ cup sweet paprika

2 tablespoons ground ginger

Vegetable oil, for frying

Tamarind Kani Sauce (page 229), for serving

These crisp, savory treats must have arrived here through the Portuguese whose own empanadas were influenced by Indian samosas. Slightly different versions, but with the same name, can be seen in former Portuguese colonies such as Brazil, Angola, and Guinea-Bissau.

For the filling, I used smoked mackerel and pickled mango (which needs to be made a few days ahead), and I crusted the dough with a spice mix before frying, a technique inspired by Brazilians, who have strong African influences in their own cooking. As a shortcut, the pastels can be prepared with the empanada dough circles found in supermarket freezers.

◉

» To prepare the dough: Bring the stock to a boil in a saucepan. Gradually stir in the flour. When the dough comes together, remove from the heat, add the salt, and continue beating until it becomes firm. Set aside to cool.

» To prepare the filling: Heat the oil in a frying pan over medium heat. Cook the onion and garlic until softened, but not browned, about 5 minutes. Let cool. Add the mackerel and cilantro and combine.

» Dust a clean work surface with flour. Divide the dough into 8 equal portions. Using a rolling pin, roll each portion of dough into a thin circle of about 5 inches in diameter and ⅛-inch thick. Cut each circle into four even triangles.

» Place about 1 tablespoon of the filling in the center of each triangle and top with a teaspoon of mango. Lightly wet the dough's edge with water, fold the straight sides of the dough together, and seal well. You may also crimp the edges with the tines of a fork.

» To prepare the spice crust: Make an egg wash by combining the 2 eggs and water in a small bowl. Combine the cayenne,

paprika, and ground ginger in a small dish. Set a few tablespoons aside for sprinkling later. Set up a station lining up the uncooked pastels, egg wash, spice mix, and a baking sheet on the end. Using one hand, dip a pastel in the egg wash, turning it to coat completely, then place it in the spice mix. Using your other hand, turn it to lightly coat. (This way, your eggy hands don't get gunked up with the spice mix.) Place the spice-coated pastel on the baking sheet. Repeat with the remaining pastels.

» Line another baking sheet or a platter with several layers of paper towels. Pour vegetable oil into a large cast-iron skillet or other heavy, straight-sided pan to a depth of 1 inch, and heat to 375°F over medium-high heat. In batches, carefully drop the pastels one at a time into the oil without crowding the pan. Gently fry over medium heat, turning once with a slotted spoon, 3 to 5 minutes each side, until golden brown. Remove with the slotted spoon and drain on the paper towels.

» Serve with more spices sprinkled over the pastels, with kani sauce on the side.

PICKLED MANGO

Makes 3 cups

2 cups water

2½ cups sugar

3 tablespoons sea salt

1 cup white vinegar

2 tablespoons cayenne pepper

4 whole cloves

2 whole selim pepper pods

2 firm, ripe mangoes, peeled, pitted, and finely diced

>> In a small pot, bring the water to a boil, then turn off the heat. Add the sugar and salt and stir to dissolve. Add the vinegar, cayenne, cloves, and selim pepper and mix well. Chill for 1 hour.

>> Pack the mangoes tightly into a sterilized 24-ounce jar. Pour the pickling liquid over the mango, filling the jar to the top. Cover tightly and store in the refrigerator for a few days until pickled to your liking. Use in the pastel filling, or enjoy as is or as a topping for salad.

SPICED CASHEWS

I always enjoyed snacking on roasted cashew nuts, which are so abundant in Casamance. This recipe was inspired from an experience a few years ago, when I consulted on recipes for a project involving Tanzanian cashews. It is quite easy to give new flavors to nuts; it can be done with almost any spice. Here, I chose the ever-popular *kan kan kan* spice. Spicy and nutty, it is most often found blanketing *dibi Hausa* (also known as *suya*), the Nigerian-style grilled meat skewers that are one of my favorite street foods. These addictive cashews can be eaten as is or used as a topping for salad (such as the Kale, Avocado & Grapefruit Salad, page 126).

1 cup raw cashew nuts
1 large egg white
1 tablespoon Kan Kan Kan Spice Mix (recipe follows)

» Preheat the oven to 350°F.

» Spread the cashews on a rimmed baking sheet and roast for 10 minutes, or until lightly browned (watch carefully, as they will burn easily). Remove from the oven (leave the oven on) and let cool.

» Combine in a large bowl the cooled cashews, egg white, and spices and mix well. Return the mixture to the baking sheet and bake for 5 more minutes. Cool completely before serving.

KAN KAN KAN SPICE MIX

Kan kan kan is traditionally used to coat the popular *dibi Hausa*. It is a wonderful dry dip for any grilled meat and fish (and also very fun to pronounce). Simply brush any meat with oil, coat it with the *kan kan kan,* and grill or roast. Serve with more *kan kan kan* as a dry dip on the side with raw onion slices.

Makes about ¾ cup

5 tablespoons peanut flour (see page 68)
2 tablespoons cayenne pepper
5 tablespoons ground ginger
2 teaspoons ground selim pepper
½ teaspoon salt
½ teaspoon freshly ground black pepper

» Combine all the ingredients. Store in an airtight container for up to 3 months.

SENEGALESE SUMMER ROLLS
with PEANUT GINGER SAUCE

This recipe is obviously inspired by the classic Vietnamese summer roll. Senegal saw a wave of Vietnamese immigrants around the time of the First Indochina War while Vietnam and Senegal were both still under French colonial rule. *Nems*, our take on fried Vietnamese spring rolls, are a beloved staple on many Senegalese menus. There's a great recipe for vegetarian *nems* in my first cookbook, *Yolele!*, but here I wanted to take a lighter route with the refreshing, healthy summer roll.

My Vietnamese uncle-godfather often prepared traditional summer rolls with shrimp or minced pork. Here is a vegetarian option with grilled eggplant, mango, carrot, and lots of fresh herbs. I also skip the rice noodles Uncle Jean used to include in his filling, and the result is a much lighter summer roll that still has all the Vietnamese flavors we love.

Be sure to have all your ingredients ready before you start rolling. If you make these ahead of time, store them on a damp towel in a covered container. Don't let the rolls touch each other or else they'll stick together.

◎

» Preheat the grill or a grill pan to hot.

» To prepare the peanut sauce: Combine all the ingredients in a small bowl and mix well. If you'd like a slightly thinner sauce, add a few more tablespoons water.

» To prepare the rolls: Trim the eggplant and cut it lengthwise into ½-inch-thick slices. Brush both sides of the eggplant slices with the olive oil and grill until cooked through, 3 to 5 minutes on each side. Let cool. Cut the eggplant into ½ by 2-inch pieces.

» Place a clean, damp kitchen towel on a plate or cutting board. Fill a wide bowl with warm water (the bowl should be large enough to dip the wrappers in).

» Immerse a wrapper in the warm water for 5 to 10 seconds, until the wrapper is pliable. Carefully lay it flat on the towel. In the center of the wrapper, place, in turn, a few leaves each of the mint, basil, and cilantro. Add a few pieces each of the mango, grilled eggplant, cucumber, scallion, and a large pinch of grated carrot. Be careful not to overfill the wrapper.

» To roll up the wrapper, fold in the left and right sides over the filling. Take the edge closest to you and tightly roll away from you, from bottom to top, like a cigar. Set the roll seam side down on a platter or baking sheet and cover with plastic wrap as you repeat with the remaining wrappers and filling.

» Serve immediately with the lettuce leaves and peanut sauce on the side. To eat, wrap a lettuce leaf around a summer roll and dip in the peanut sauce.

PEANUT GINGER SAUCE
- ¾ cup unsweetened smooth peanut butter
- 1 tablespoon peeled, grated fresh ginger
- 2 tablespoons water
- 3 tablespoons honey
- 1 tablespoon lime juice
- ¼ cup soy sauce
- 1 teaspoon Vietnamese or Thai fish sauce
- 1 teaspoon tamarind paste
- 1 garlic clove, minced
- ½ teaspoon toasted sesame oil
- ½ teaspoon cayenne pepper

ROLLS
- 2 medium Japanese eggplants
- Extra virgin olive oil, for brushing
- 16 (8½-inch) round rice paper wrappers
- 1 bunch mint, leaves only
- 1 bunch basil, leaves only
- 1 bunch cilantro, leaves only
- 1 ripe mango, peeled and cut into ¼ by 2-inch pieces
- 1 Kirby cucumber, peeled and cut into ¼ by 2-inch pieces
- 3 scallions, cut lengthwise into 2-inch pieces
- 1 carrot, peeled and coarsely grated
- 1 head Boston lettuce, leaves separated

SWEET-SPICY PALM OIL POPCORN

¼ **cup red palm oil**

½ **cup sugar**

½ **cup popcorn kernels**

2 **tablespoons Kan Kan Kan Spice Mix (page 87)**

2 **tablespoons grated lime zest**

My kids love this sweet-spicy popcorn. Melting the sugar into the red palm oil balances the heat of the *kan kan kan* spices, while the lime zest at the end gives it a fresh pop. If you're looking for an easy way to add palm oil to your diet, this is it.

» Heat the oil and sugar in a large saucepan (with a lid) over medium heat, stirring with a wooden spoon until the sugar dissolves.

» Add the popcorn kernels and stir to coat. Tightly cover the pan and let the popping begin. When the sound of the popping starts to diminish, remove the pan from the heat and keep it covered until the popping stops.

» Transfer the hot popcorn to a large bowl and toss with the spices and lime zest. Serve immediately.

TAMARIND LITTLENECK CLAMS

SERVES
4

A t school, come recess, women selling all kinds of snacks would line up their enamel platters on straw mats alongside the Sacré-Coeur School's wall, and the kids would flock to them. With 25 francs, I could get *paañ niambaan*, a dish of sun-dried littleneck clams, fresh onion, lime, cayenne pepper, and tamarind served on kraft paper. It was another one of my favorite street foods growing up. This version, prepared with fresh clams, is my loving throwback to that school-day favorite.

4 pounds littleneck clams (discard any clams that remain open after pressed with fingers)

1 cup Spicy Tamarind Glaze (page 192)

1 cup water

16 fresh Thai or regular basil leaves, thinly sliced

2 scallions, thinly sliced

2 limes, cut into wedges

◉

» To clean the clams, rinse under cold running water and scrub each clam with a brush to remove the sand.

» In a large saucepan with a tightly fitting lid, combine the tamarind glaze and water and bring to a boil. Add the clams and cover. Cook over medium heat and remove the clams as they open, 5 to 7 minutes. Discard any clams that don't open.

» Drizzle the pan juices over the clams and top with the basil and scallions. Serve immediately with the lime wedges on the side.

DAKAR, A RIOT OF COLOR, FLAVORS, AND SOUND

Located on a peninsula, Dakar is a tale of two cities. The downtown bustles with its glass towers, gleaming luxury cars, and elegantly dressed people next to beggars, street hustlers, horse-cart drivers, and the occasional herd of unattended cattle stopping traffic. Hip and colorful, Dakar fashion could put Paris or Milan to shame. Usually slim and tall, Dakarois have the striking look of models, and people love to dress up in colorful traditional outfits, fitted tailored attire, or the latest fashion. Compared to the rest of Senegal, the pulse of Dakar moves at a different beat altogether.

Between the unending cacophony of horns from desperate taxi drivers directed at every potential client, there are the loud radios playing *mbalax* music, local hip hop, or talk shows from passing *car rapides*; the inevitable beggars chanting Arabic and Wolof prayers at streetlights for food or change; and the constant buzz of people laughing, chatting, or haggling in the streets and offices. Dakar is loud and colorful and fun, but this vibrant city is above all rich with its people.

The food culture of Dakar reflects this city of contrasts: fancy restaurants on the avenues that serve mostly French cuisine compete with popular Lebanese shawarma joints, Vietnamese-influenced restaurants, and a fascinating street-food scene. Food for all budgets is available at any time, day or night. There are underground neighborhood restaurants called *maquis* (my favorite hangouts) that specialize in local and subregional cuisines from our West African neighbors, filling our bellies with the verdant *ndolé* stews of Cameroon, the fine Ivorian *attiéké* (cassava couscous) that soaks up our stews, and Nigerian *dibi Hausa*, grilled skewers of lamb dusted with an addictive dry peanut-spice powder. An even cheaper way to have a taste of Dakar is from the ever-present street food. There is always a *gargote*-style *tangana,* a simple stall selling local snacks for a quick bite.

BLACK-EYED PEA FRITTER SANDWICHES

with SPICY PICKLED CARROTS

MAKES
4
SANDWICHES

Accara, black-eyed pea fritters, can be found on many street corners of West Africa and Brazil, where they are called *acarajé*. Although baguettes are more common in Senegal, I prefer to use pita here for a spin on the classic falafel sandwich, a nod to the Lebanese community of Dakar. The sweet and spicy pickled carrots and cilantro—inspired by another Senegalese immigrant group, the Vietnamese—bring the customary heat to the *accara* fritters, confirming a popular Wolof saying: *"Ku beuggeu accara daye gneme kani,"* meaning, "You must stand the heat if you want *accara*."

1 cup dried black-eyed peas
2 tablespoons chopped onion
½ teaspoon baking soda
½ teaspoon fine sea salt
Vegetable oil, for frying
4 pita breads
Spicy Pickled Carrots (recipe follows), for serving

TOPPINGS
Lettuce leaves
Sliced tomatoes
Sliced red onion
Fresh cilantro leaves

>> Place the black-eyed peas in a large bowl with enough warm water to cover. Soak for 10 to 15 minutes, until the skins easily peel off when rubbed between the palms of your hands. Rub the skins off the peas, letting the skins float to the top. Slowly pour out the water and the skins with it, leaving the peas in the bowl. Repeat until all the peas are cleaned.

>> Drain the peas and place in a food processor along with the onion, baking soda, salt, and a splash of water. Process until a smooth batter forms, adding a little more water if necessary. The batter should be smooth and light, similar to the consistency of light hummus.

>> Pour oil into a large cast-iron skillet or other heavy, straight-sided pan to a depth of 1 inch, and heat to 365°F over medium-high heat. Reduce the heat to medium and using a spoon, carefully drop 1 tablespoon of batter into the oil. Repeat until there are several dollops in the pan, being careful not to overcrowd it. Fry until golden brown, turning the fritters once. Remove with a slotted spoon and set aside. Repeat until all the batter is used.

>> Stuff each pita bread with 3 or 4 fritters, a generous spoonful of pickled carrots, and some lettuce, tomato, onion, and cilantro. Serve immediately.

SPICY PICKLED CARROTS

This spicy-sweet-tart pickle is of my godfather's Vietnamese roots. Uncle Jean prepared his with jalapeno, but I find it works very well with Scotch bonnet, too. It is an excellent condiment to add a spicy fresh kick to any meal.

Makes about 3 cups

6 carrots, peeled and coarsely grated
1 Scotch bonnet pepper, seeded and finely chopped
½ yellow onion, finely chopped
1 tablespoon salt
1 cup packed light brown sugar
2 cups rice vinegar

)) In a large bowl, combine the carrots, Scotch bonnet, onion, and salt and let sit for about 1 hour to draw out excess liquid.

)) Drain the water from the vegetables and place them in a pot with the sugar and vinegar. Bring to a boil, then remove from the heat. Keep the pot covered, off the heat, for about 15 minutes. Pack in sterilized jars, seal, and let cool. Store in the refrigerator for up to 3 weeks. Drain before serving as a side or condiment.

Dakar Dakar Dakar Dakaaar!!!
Wakam Wakam Wakam Wakaaam!!!
Pikine Pikine Pikine Pikiiine!!!!

SAY A PRAYER, HOP IN IF YOU DARE

This is a familiar soundtrack and sight to anyone who lives in Dakar. The loud syncopated voice belongs to the *apprenti*, a boy hanging carelessly from the swinging back door of a *car rapide*, repeatedly announcing the destinations of these cool-looking, colorfully painted vans that crisscross the streets of Dakar.

Taking a *car rapide*, which translates to "fast bus," is the cheapest way to travel in Dakar as long as you don't mind being crushed between passengers in a jam-packed minibus. You may also get startled and jump with surprise a few times when the driver suddenly hits the brakes either to pick a passenger up or because someone loudly banged on the side of the minibus to request a stop. (The proper way to request a stop is to signal the *apprenti*, who will knock on the van's roof with a coin.)

For less than 200 CFA (about 40 cents USD), you can get a ride to your destination. Of course, there are no designated stops for *car rapides*. To get to where you want to go, just flag one, ask the *apprenti* the general direction they're going, say a prayer, and hop in if you dare—be aware that the *car rapide* may still be in motion while passengers are getting on and off.

Riding a *rapide* is also a great way to get immersed in Dakar culture. There is always good conversation to be had, the topic of which depends on who is sitting near you, since all types of people ride *car rapides*.

Yellow and blue, each *car rapide* is uniquely adorned with paintings, quotes, and prayers that identify, depending on the owner's religious affiliation, the name of one of the two major holy cities of the country: Touba or Tivaouane, the capital of the Tiijaniya Sufi group. *"Bonne Maman"* (Good Mom), *"Dieu est Grand"* (God is Great), or *"Alhamdulillah"* (Praise Allah) are a few other most familiar *car rapide* writings.

However, these prayers don't always seem to work, considering the number of accidents involving *car rapides*. The driver may not have a proper license or car registration, but a few bills for the police officer will often do. A few years ago, *car rapides* were deemed unsafe and declared illegal because of the high rate of traffic accidents. No matter, they are still very much present in the city.

A somewhat safer way to travel in Dakar is by taxi. Of course, only if you don't mind a broken windshield or being able to see the pavement from your seat. You must always remember to bargain before getting in the taxi. For a good bargainer, the taxi fare shouldn't cost more than 2,000 CFA (about $4 USD).

KILISHI GREEN MANGO SALAD

SERVES
4

DRESSING

1 tablespoon rice vinegar

1 garlic clove, chopped

1 tablespoon sugar

Juice of 1 lime

2 tablespoons Vietnamese or
    Thai fish sauce

SALAD

2 large green mangoes,
    peeled

1 teaspoon sugar

2 to 3 tablespoons coarse salt

1 cup Kilishi (recipe follows)

¼ cup thinly sliced red onion

¼ cup fresh basil leaves cut
    into thin ribbons

Salt and freshly ground black
    pepper

Kilishi is the popular Hausa beef jerky. Of nomadic origins, the Hausa people certainly began drying meat because it was convenient for long days on the road in search of greener pastures. This refreshing salad is a nod to my Vietnamese godfather's traditional green mango and beef jerky salad (*goi du du kho bo*)—it has all the bright flavors of Vietnam we love, but with an African twist in the earthy *kilishi* and spicy *kani*. Please note that the *kilishi* needs to be marinated overnight.

◉

》 To prepare the dressing: Combine all the ingredients in a small bowl and whisk until the sugar dissolves.

》 To prepare the salad: Shred the mangoes using the largest holes of a box grater, discarding the seed, or thinly julienne by hand. Place the mango in a colander, add the sugar and salt, and toss to combine. Let sit for about 30 minutes; the mango will lose some of its moisture and appear limp. Rinse well under cold running water to remove the salt and sugar.

》 Using a clean dishtowel or your hands, carefully wring out the moisture from the mango without crushing the fruit. Transfer to a bowl.

》 Just before serving, add the beef jerky, red onion, and basil to the mango and toss to combine. Add dressing to taste, toss well, and adjust the seasoning. Serve immediately.

KILISHI (HAUSA BEEF JERKY)

Traditionally, *kilishi* is dried in the hot sun for 2 to 3 days. This is the home version that can be done in a low oven in about 4 hours. To make cutting the beef into thin strips easier, freeze the meat partway before cutting. Be aware that the beef must marinate overnight.

Makes about 4 cups

3 tablespoons raw peanuts
1 pound boneless beef top round, cut into thin ⅛-inch-thick strips
1 teaspoon cayenne pepper
1 tablespoon vegetable oil
Pinch of salt

》 In a coffee or spice grinder, grind the peanuts to a fine meal. You don't want it to become peanut butter, so be careful not to grind it excessively. In a large bowl, combine the ground peanuts, beef, cayenne, oil, and salt and mix well. Cover and marinate overnight in the refrigerator.

》 Preheat the oven to 160°F.

》 Arrange the beef strips in a single layer on wire racks set on top of baking sheets. Make sure you don't overlap the strips so that air can circulate well around them. Place in the oven to dehydrate. Check after 4 hours. The strips should be chewy and tender. If they aren't yet, return to the oven and check every 15 minutes until done.

》 Let the jerky cool on the racks. Blot with paper towels to dry before storing in a tightly sealed container in the refrigerator. The jerky will keep, refrigerated, for up to 2 months.

HERB-STUFFED JOLLOF CROQUETTES

This twist on arancini (Italian rice balls) came from my friend Carole, who wanted me to prepare the perennial Senegalese favorite, *thiebou jenn*, as a finger food for her cocktail party. These rice balls are stuffed with *rof,* a parsley mixture traditionally used to stuff the fish in *thiebou jenn*. I crisp them in a hot oven so the outside gets a crunchy texture reminiscent of *khogn*, the delicious crisp rice that forms at the bottom of the *thiebou jenn* pot. Here I use leftover Vegetarian Jollof Rice (page 165) to keep it vegetarian-friendly, but you can also use the rice leftover from *thiebou jenn*. Whatever rice you choose, it's a fun party food that can be made ahead of time, then baked when you want to serve.

1 tablespoon vegetable oil, plus more for greasing the baking sheet

1 cup cooked Vegetarian Jollof Rice (page 165) or Thiebou Jenn rice (page 204)

1 cup cooked fonio (page 150) or quinoa

1 tablespoon tomato paste

½ cup vegetable stock

1 teaspoon freshly ground black pepper

½ cup Rof (page 207)

Tamarind Kani Sauce (page 229), for serving

» Preheat the oven to 375°F. Lightly oil a large baking sheet.

» In a large bowl, combine the rice and fonio; mix well. In a small saucepan, heat the oil over medium heat. Add the tomato paste and reduce the heat to low. Cook, stirring frequently, for about 10 minutes, until the paste is dark red. If necessary, add a little bit of water or vegetable stock from time to time to avoid burning.

» Add the stock and stir well to combine. Bring to a boil, then reduce the heat and simmer for 15 to 20 minutes, until thick enough to coat the back of a spoon. Season with the pepper and remove from the heat. Gradually add to the rice and fonio a tablespoon at a time, mixing as you go, until the grains are moist and thick enough to compact into a ball, but not too wet or dry to fall apart. Set aside to cool.

» Using your hands, shape a few tablespoons of the cooled grains into little oval balls about the size of an oblong ping-pong ball. Make an indentation in the center of each with your thumb and stuff with a generous pinch of the rof. Carefully enclose the herbs inside and rework the grains into a smooth ball. Place on the prepared baking sheet. Repeat with the remaining grains.

» Bake the balls for 10 to 15 minutes, until lightly browned and crisp. Serve hot with the kani sauce on the side.

DAKAR 'TIL DAWN

"Dakar ne dort pas!" is the slogan of a popular television show in Senegal that translates to "Dakar never sleeps!" and indeed this city is always lively. Of course, with any vibrant night culture, an equally exciting late-night food culture goes hand in hand.

Often on weekends in the early evening, neighborhoods organize a *sabar*, which to me is an amazing concept. A *sabar* is the ultimate drum and dance street party: people simply get together and jam. Neighborhoods close down an entire block, bring drummers, and dance—and what a dance it is! They are the most rhythmically syncopated moves you'll ever get to experience. It's part of the beauty of Senegal—street dances are a regular thing and everyone gets down!

The Dakar club scene doesn't really start getting hot before midnight. That's when people start pouring into the clubs to dance or listen to live music. One of my favorite hangouts, Just4U, is located just around the corner from where I grew up. It's where I go to listen to incredible live music and have a fun time with my buddies. Awadi, arguably one of the pillars of the African-conscious hip-hop movement, often performs here when he is not traveling the world.

At night, formal restaurants compete with neighborhood joints commonly nicknamed *maquis*, which actually is a term that designates a place where the armed resistance of a guerilla movement takes refuge. Most *maquis* serve Ivorian, Cameroonian, or other West African specialties. These underground hangouts are usually unpretentious, loud, and fun. The decor is casual and the ambiance always jovial. Dakar people are very friendly and there is always an opportunity for great conversations with the people sitting next to you.

Late nights after partying, *dibiteries* serving great-tasting wood-fired lamb or goat barbecue are legion. *Dibiteries* are very popular and affordable hangouts, and they get packed. The grilled meat is fresh and served either in a crusty baguette or on a platter with your choice of french fries or fried plantains, mustard and chile jam on the side.

Dakar, being a peninsula, has lots of beachside shacks or sometimes just tables placed right on the beach next to makeshift drum barrel grills glowing with wood charcoal. The charcoal is made from burning wood under piles of earth, and despite its popularity in Senegal, this practice is unfortunately not very good for the environment. Thus, the authorities came up with a compromise, and now people need permits to trade wood charcoal. Hefty fines are given to those caught in the illegal trafficking of wood for charcoal and the *gendarmerie* (interstate police) often seize charcoal bags from people when they have more than their authorized limit of one bag per car.

The grills are manned by vendors with stalls full of freshly caught fish, huge spider lobsters, shrimp of all sizes, sea urchins, oysters, clams, and more. These candlelit places are among my favorite destinations on hot Dakar nights. You just point your finger at the fish or seafood that you want to eat and

the vendor prepares it for you while you sit at the table right on the beach. The perfect place to go for this type of beach shack is La Pointe, an area located behind the US embassy at the edge of Dakar, overlooking the Atlantic.

Bakeries are always a late-night option and a reminder that the French are still a big part of our culture. Many of the bakeries are open all night, serving great pastries, croissants, and sandwiches on baguettes and brioche. New bakeries opening in many neighborhoods beyond the downtown area have become a welcome addition to the food scene. Among my favorites are franchises of the Brioche Dorée patisserie and sandwicherie, and Eric Kayser's artisanal bakery.

Dakar nights wouldn't be the same without the necessary last stop: the *tangana*. These affordable shacks that specialize in breakfast are where people in the know hit up in the wee hours of the morning. *Maiga* is the nickname of the person who runs a *tangana*—like a generic "Joe." One of the *maiga*'s specialties is a delicious homemade coffee drink with sweetened condensed milk, similar to Vietnamese coffee. He deftly stirs the coffee with a long spoon in a cadenced up-and-down movement as he slowly pours the milk into the coffee glass, creating foam. In *tanganas*, this sweet coffee is always served with fresh baguette sandwiches stuffed with various fillings such as butter, omelets, grilled lamb skewers, or bean stew. All this costs about 1,000 CFA, less than $2.00 USD.

"Dakar never goes hungry!" should really be the sister slogan to "Dakar never sleeps!"

GINGER-LIME PEANUT HUMMUS

¼ cup plus 2 tablespoons olive oil

½ yellow onion, finely chopped

1 garlic clove, minced

1 tablespoon peeled, minced fresh ginger

1 Scotch bonnet pepper, seeded and finely chopped

2 cups shelled Salted Boiled Peanuts (recipe follows)

Juice of 2 limes

Salt and freshly ground black pepper

2 tablespoons chopped fresh cilantro

This dish was inspired by chickpea hummus because when boiled, chickpeas remind me of the boiled peanuts that I loved to eat in Casamance at my grandmother's. The peanuts must be boiled until very soft before they are mashed and combined with the other ingredients. This flavor-packed dip is delicious with chips or crudités. Make sure you don't add the cilantro until serving, as it will brown.

» In a large frying pan, heat 2 tablespoons of the oil over medium heat. Add the onion and slowly cook until just soft, stirring continuously; do not let it brown. Add the garlic and ginger and cook for about 1 minute more. Add the Scotch bonnet and peanuts and mix well. Add the lime juice and bring to a boil. Reduce the heat and simmer for about 5 minutes, until the liquid is absorbed. Set aside to cool.

» Place about two-thirds of the peanut mixture in a food processor and add the remaining ¼ cup oil. Process until smooth. Season to taste with salt and pepper.

» Transfer the purée to a bowl and fold in the remaining peanut mixture. Right before serving, fold in the cilantro. Enjoy with chips, bread, or cut-up raw vegetables.

SALTED BOILED PEANUTS

To me, boiled peanuts spell summer at Grand-Mère's in Ziguinchor, when peanuts abound. This is one of my favorite ways to eat peanuts.

Makes 2 cups

1 pound raw peanuts, in the shell

¼ cup sea salt

1 quart water

» In a large pot, bring the peanuts, salt, and water to a boil. Reduce the heat to medium and simmer for at least 3 hours, until the peanuts are very soft. Drain and let cool until you can handle them.

» Shell and enjoy. Store in the refrigerator for up to 2 days.

CRYSTALLIZED PEANUTS

This wonderful snack can be found everywhere in the streets of Dakar. In my version, these sweet, crunchy nuts get a pop of brightness from the lime zest and nice heat from the cayenne. They make a delicious snack as is, or for a special treat, coarsely crush them and sprinkle over your favorite ice cream like a textured praline topping.

2 cups shelled raw peanuts
1½ cups water
2 cups sugar
Grated zest of 2 limes
2 teaspoons cayenne pepper

» In a dry cast-iron skillet, pan-roast the peanuts over medium heat until golden, occasionally shaking the pan, about 15 minutes.

» Meanwhile, combine the water and sugar in a small saucepan and bring to a boil over medium heat. When it forms a syrup and begins to color, add the peanuts. Whisk until they are coated and the syrup starts to crystallize on them.

» Using a slotted spoon, transfer the peanuts to a wide platter and spread them out, making sure they don't stick together. Sprinkle the lime zest and cayenne over the peanuts and let cool, stirring occasionally to prevent sticking. Store in an airtight container for up to 6 months.

POP FONIO

MAKES ABOUT
2
CUPS

2 cups cooked fonio (page 150), cooled to room temperature

1 cup peanut, vegetable, or red palm oil

Fine sea salt

Togo and Benin form a strong community in Senegal. As West African neighbors, there are similarities in their cuisines and much of the street food in Senegal, including *talé talé* (banana beignets) and *accara* (page 101), originates from them. This snack was inspired by the women of southern Togo who, as in much of rural West Africa, grow *fonio*. Pop *fonio* is a popular snack there and I love its unique crunchy, nutty taste, especially when sprinkled over salads.

◉

❯❯ Preheat the oven to 175°F. Line a large baking sheet with parchment paper.

❯❯ Spread the fonio in a single layer on the baking sheet. Bake the fonio for about 2 hours, until dry. Shake the pan once or twice while baking to ensure it is evenly dried.

❯❯ Line a baking sheet or platter with several layers of paper towels. Pour the oil into a large cast-iron skillet or other heavy, straight-sided pan and heat to 350°F over medium-high heat.

❯❯ Carefully fry the fonio in small batches. Once the fonio puffs and floats to the surface, remove with a fine-mesh sieve and drain on the paper towels. Season with salt. Serve warm or at room temperature. It can be stored in an airtight container in the refrigerator for up to 2 months.

OPPOSITE: The calabash is a kitchen tool with deep spiritual dimensions. Just like the mortar and pestle, the calabash or bottle gourd is part of daily life everywhere in Africa. When harvested as a hard-shelled mature fruit, the calabash becomes a practical kitchen tool, an all-purpose container or ladle, depending on its size and shape. Its voluptuous, rounded bowl can also be turned into a musical instrument and in some African cultures, calabashes are used ceremonially as symbols of fertility.

Wherever you stand in Dakar, you will notice the towering and rather controversial statue dedicated to the African Renaissance. This *gigantesque* sculpture, taller than the Statue of Liberty, is deplored by most people here and considered a waste of money. Although it was meant to symbolize the African Renaissance, the statue representing a man, a woman, and their child pointing with his finger toward the horizon was built by North Koreans and has a Stalin-era appearance.

The scantily dressed woman with a sarong wrapped around her, partially revealing a breast, was seen by some as inappropriate in this majority Muslim country. The resilient Dakarois population seems at last to have come to terms with the fact that the statue is here to stay, and so they prefer to crack jokes about it rather than think of ways to blow it up. One of my favorite comments is that the kid on the statue is pointing his finger to show the way to the desperate dugout boats full of immigrants on their way to Europe for better living conditions.

THE INFAMOUS STATUE

VEGETABLES

KALE, AVOCADO & GRAPEFRUIT SALAD
(SALADE CASAMANCE)

5 ounces baby kale

1 avocado, thinly sliced

1 cup grapefruit segments (see Note; save the membranes)

½ red onion, thinly sliced

1 teaspoon Dijon mustard

1 garlic clove, minced

Fine sea salt and freshly ground black pepper

¼ cup extra virgin olive oil

½ cup roasted unsalted cashew nuts, coarsely chopped

G reat to pack for summer picnics or barbecues, this salad can be eaten on its own or served as a side to grilled meats.

» Place the kale, avocado, grapefruit segments, and red onion in a large bowl and gently toss.

» In a bowl, squeeze all the juice out of the membranes of the grapefruit. Add the mustard, garlic, and salt and pepper to taste and whisk well. Slowly add the oil, whisking constantly to emulsify.

» To serve, fold the dressing into the salad. Top with the cashews.

NOTE: *Citrus segments without the peel and membrane are called* suprêmes *(a French culinary term). To supreme the grapefruit (or any other citrus fruit), first slice ¼ to ½ inch off the top and bottom. Place the fruit on its bottom and from the top down, begin to pare away the peel and pith (the white part), following the curve and leaving as much fruit flesh as possible. Once all the peel and pith are gone, remove the segments by slicing into the flesh close to either side of the membranes, working all around the fruit. When removing the segments, hold the fruit over a bowl to catch any juices. In this case, save the remains to squeeze into the dressing for the salad.*

RAW COLLARD GREENS SALAD

with SWEET POTATOES, MANGO & GOAT CHEESE

SERVES
4

Brother Simon Sarr is spearheading a food revolution with the use of local products at the small Keur Moussa Monastery in Senegal (see page 268). They make cashew apple liqueur, hibiscus wines, baobab seed oil, and plenty of fruit spreads. Among my favorite products is their goat cheese, prepared from the milk collected by local Fulani herders. It has a particularly rich, smooth taste that perfectly complements this healthy, colorful salad tossed in a ginger-spiked dressing.

◉

» To prepare the sweet potatoes: Preheat the oven to 400°F. In a large bowl, combine all the ingredients and toss well. Spread in a single layer on a rimmed baking sheet. Roast until tender and slightly charred, 30 to 40 minutes, turning over the pieces with a spatula about halfway through. Set aside to cool.

» To prepare the dressing: In a bowl, combine the lime juice, ginger, 1 teaspoon salt, and ½ teaspoon pepper, whisking to dissolve the salt. Add the palm oil, whisking constantly to emulsify. Adjust the seasoning if necessary.

» To prepare the salad: Place the collard greens in a large salad bowl and sprinkle with a tablespoon of the dressing. Gently massage for a few minutes, until soft and wilted. Add the sweet potatoes and mangoes and toss well. Drizzle the remaining dressing and crumble the goat cheese over the salad. Top with cashews (if using) and serve immediately.

ROASTED SWEET POTATOES
- 2 sweet potatoes, peeled and cut into ½-inch cubes
- 1 tablespoon fresh thyme leaves, finely chopped
- 1 tablespoon cumin seeds
- 2 tablespoons red palm oil or vegetable oil
- 2 garlic cloves, lightly crushed with the side of a knife
- ½ teaspoon salt

GINGER DRESSING
- 2 tablespoons fresh lime juice
- 1 teaspoon peeled, chopped fresh ginger
- Fine sea salt and freshly ground black pepper
- ¼ cup red palm oil or vegetable oil

SALAD
- ½ bunch collard greens, tough ribs removed, leaves roughly torn
- 2 mangoes, peeled, pitted, and cut into ½-inch cubes
- ¼ cup fresh goat cheese
- ¼ cup roasted unsalted cashew nuts, coarsely chopped (optional)

RED GOLD

My parents grew up in Casamance, the region that produces most of the red palm oil in Senegal. Maman would use it in many different ways: as a side condiment, simply drizzled over *thiebou diola*, a dish consisting of *nyankatang* (white rice) steamed together with *nététou* (fermented locust beans), grilled fish, and *baguedj* (sorrel and okra sauce), or in more elaborate dishes such as *soupou kandja*, the okra-and-seafood-laden stew that became known as gumbo in Southern cooking in America. At home, red palm oil was also prized for its healing properties. My grandmother was a firm believer in red palm oil as medicine. Whenever someone was sick she would suggest drinking a couple of tablespoons of the red stuff.

Red palm oil is involved in one way or another with some of the best meals in my memory. I still use it in my kitchen, just as I would butter, bacon fat, or other vegetable oils, and I even use it for frying. It has a distinct earthy flavor that some find is an acquired taste.

This special red oil, which has been used in African cooking for thousands of years, has become one of the most controversial foods at the moment. The palm oil debate stirs up a lot of passion and I find myself in the unique position of being an advocate for both red palm oil use and environmental consciousness.

RED PALM OIL VERSUS PALM KERNEL OIL

It is important to distinguish red palm oil from palm kernel oil. Although both are processed from the same fruit, red palm oil is derived from the pulp of the palm fruit, while the kernel oil is extracted from the fruit's kernel. Unlike highly processed, colorless palm kernel oil, red palm oil has a deep orange color derived from the fruit itself, and is one of the highest natural sources for beta-carotene (which also gives carrots and sweet potatoes their orange color). It is also rich in vitamin A, vitamin E, and antioxidants. According to some studies, red palm oil may even lower cholesterol and help maintain proper blood pressure.

When cooking with palm oil, it is extremely important to know which one to use. Always look for virgin red palm oil that's been extracted naturally, without industrial hydrogenation, as has been done for countless generations in small villages such as Etoufane, my friend Diallo's village in Casamance. Ever since trans fats were banned by the FDA, many large corporations have turned to the unhealthy hydrogenated palm kernel oil as its replacement in highly processed foods.

In addition, for the sake of palm oil profits, irreplaceable forests are being destroyed in Southeast Asia and Central Africa. This environmental crime should be condemned. There is no need to destroy forests when there are millions of acres of arable land in degraded savanna or agricultural areas that can be converted to grow palm fruit trees. The conscious consumer should look for palm oil sourced from small farmers, which is mainly the case in regions such as West Africa.

SENEGALESE SPOTLIGHT:

Diallo, a Diola Palm Oil Producer in Casamance

Diallo is a muscular octogenarian palm oil producer whose incredibly fit body is the incarnation of health. He is of mixed Diola and Fulani heritage (just like me) and lives in a remote Casamance village located a few kilometers' drive on dirt roads from the town of Oussouye.

Despite his advanced age, Diallo still climbs trees as tall as fifty feet to cut palm fruit bunches with a machete. Each bunch can easily weigh more than 10 kilograms (22 pounds) and contain over 1,000 bright red marble-size fruits. Once he makes his way down from the tree, Diallo separates the fruits from the bunch with his machete. He then puts the loose palm fruits in a giant iron pot sitting over burning wood logs. He adds enough water to cover the fruits and brings it to a boil.

The cooked palm fruit is then strained and transferred to a huge wooden mortar. With help from his teen-aged granddaughters, Diallo pounds the fruits vigorously until they turn into a red blend that is returned to the big pot, covered with more water, and cooked at a slow simmer. After some time, the red palm oil begins rising to the surface of the water and Diallo slowly scoops it into jerry cans to be sold at the market.

Nothing is wasted. The remaining palm fruit water is strained and used to prepare stews with greens and smoked catfish. The strained fibers are mixed with honey or sugar and shaped into small balls, a treat the kids adore. The remaining hard black kernels are given to roaming pigs, and the leftover fiber to the chicken and ducks wandering freely around the village.

Diallo's oil is wholesome; there is no hydrogenation involved. In his village, palm trees graciously grow in the surrounding forest among a diversity of other trees. This is the prototype of red palm oil production that ought be supported for the sake of the environment and our own well-being.

SALAD OF ROASTED BEETS

with CASHEW PURÉE, COCOA NIBS & SELIM PEPPER

SERVES
4

AUTHOR'S NOTE:

This recipe is from my dear friend, the very talented chef Anita Lo. I met Anita, whose food I love, at the 11th Havana Biennial when we were guest chefs for the Proyecto Paladar *art project.*

16 baby beets of various colors, trimmed (save the tops for another use)

Vegetable oil, for coating the beets

Salt and freshly ground black pepper

CASHEW PURÉE

½ cup roasted, salted cashew nuts

VINAIGRETTE

2 tablespoons fresh lemon juice

6 tablespoons vegetable oil

SCALLION OIL (OPTIONAL)

1 bunch scallions, greens only

1 cup vegetable oil

Large pinch of toasted, ground selim pepper

1 tablespoon cocoa nibs

1 candy cane beet, peeled and very thinly sliced on a mandoline

1 orange or golden beet, peeled and very thinly sliced on a mandoline

I was one of the lucky few chefs invited to participate in the first annual AfroEats festival in Senegal, led by Chef Pierre. I not only came away with memories of a beautiful country, but some lasting friendships and this recipe, which I am still serving at my New York City restaurant, annisa.

All over Dakar were little carts selling café Touba—a powerful mix of coffee, sugar, and spices. One of the spices used in café Touba is *selim* pepper, locally known as *djar*, which adds peppery, earthy, and somewhat smoky and floral notes. I brought back a small sample to play with, and enlisted my friend, spice maestro Lior Lev Sercarz of La Boîte to source it for me here. The beets and cocoa nibs are a perfect match for the earthy tones of the pepper, and as cashews, beets, and chocolate all grow in West Africa, the combination naturally works. —*Anita Lo, annisa*

◉

» Preheat the oven to 400°F.

» Scrub the beets and dry them thoroughly. Toss with a little oil to coat, season with salt and pepper, and wrap in aluminum foil. Bake until a knife is easily inserted into the fattest portion of a beet, 30 to 45 minutes. Let the beets cool until they are easy to handle. Peel, starting with the lightest colored beets and wearing disposable gloves, if possible. Keep the dark red beets separate so they don't bleed into the others.

» **To prepare the cashew purée:** Place the cashews in a blender with water to cover and purée until smooth. Taste and adjust the seasoning. Blend in more cashews or water to create a thick, spreadable, yet puddling purée.

» **To prepare the vinaigrette:** Whisk together the lemon juice and oil until combined. Taste and season with salt and pepper.

» **To prepare the scallion oil (if using):** Bring a pot of salted water to a boil and set up an ice bath. Blanch the scallion greens for 1 minute, until they are limp but still bright green. Drain and place in the ice bath until cold. Squeeze dry, removing as much water as possible. Purée the scallions with the oil in a blender until smooth, but don't let it heat up. Strain through a fine-mesh sieve lined with damp cheesecloth. Taste and adjust the seasoning.

» To serve, quarter the roasted beets. Season with salt, black pepper, and selim pepper and toss with vinaigrette (toss the dark beets separately). Place a large spoonful of cashew purée on each plate and decorate with cocoa nibs. Arrange the seasoned beets on top. Garnish the plate with a small amount of the scallion oil (if desired) and garnish the roasted beets with slices of raw beets. Serve immediately.

MORINGA VEGGIE BURGER

with YASSA ONIONS

Veggie burgers don't have to be tasteless to be healthy. This one has the advantage of being packed with flavor as well as protein. The caramelized *yassa* onions add a mild tart-sweetness and make a great topping. This burger can be eaten with buns, lettuce, and tomato like a regular burger or if you wish, skip the buns and serve it with a salad or yuca fries (page 212).

» Place the yuca in a pot and cover with salted water. Bring to a boil, then reduce the heat to medium. Cook until the yuca is very soft, about 20 minutes. Drain well and let cool until it is easy to handle. Remove and discard the string-like fibrous core.

» Mash the yuca in a large bowl. Add the fonio, moringa, shallots, thyme, parsley, salt, and pepper. Using your hands, mix well until the filling holds together. Shape into 4 burgers and place on a plate. Cover with plastic wrap and refrigerate for about 1 hour to firm up.

» Heat the oil in a large nonstick pan over medium-high heat. Cook the burgers for 5 to 7 minutes on each side, until nicely golden brown. Serve hot in the toasted buns, topped with yassa onions, lettuce, tomato, and kani sauce.

½ **pound yuca, peeled and cut into large chunks**

1 **cup cooked fonio (page 150) or quinoa**

1 **cup finely chopped moringa leaves or fresh spinach**

2 **shallots, finely chopped**

1 **tablespoon fresh thyme leaves, finely chopped**

1 **tablespoon fresh parsley, finely chopped**

2 **teaspoons salt**

1 **teaspoon freshly ground black pepper**

2 **tablespoons vegetable oil**

4 **burger buns, toasted**

TOPPINGS

Yassa Onions (page 232)

Lettuce leaves

Sliced tomatoes

Tamarind Kani Sauce (page 229)

GARLICKY MOJO
ROOT VEGETABLE SALAD

1 pound yuca, peeled and cut into large chunks

½ pound whole okra pods, trimmed

½ cup olive oil, plus more for the okra

2 cups roasted sweet potatoes (page 129)

8 garlic cloves, finely chopped

½ small red onion, thinly sliced

Juice of 2 limes

2 teaspoons salt

1 teaspoon freshly ground black pepper

On a trip to Cuba, I was delighted to see that Cubans share many similarities with the Senegalese, particularly when it comes to their food products. Havana's farmers' markets abound with the same fresh produce seen in Dakar's—*moringa*, sweet potatoes, yuca, okra, and Scotch bonnets, to name a few. I fell in love with the way Cubans prepare yuca, simply boiled and served with a lemon and garlic dressing (*mojo criollo*), and added my own Senegalese twist here.

◉

❱❱ Place the yuca in a large pot and cover with salted water. Bring to a boil, then reduce the heat to medium. Cook until the yuca is tender but not falling apart, about 15 minutes. Drain well and let cool until it is easy to handle. Remove and discard the string-like fibrous core. Cut the yuca into ½-inch cubes and place in a large heatproof bowl.

❱❱ Preheat the grill or a grill pan to hot. Toss the okra with a little oil and grill until charred on all sides, 3 to 5 minutes. Add the okra to the bowl of yuca along with the sweet potatoes.

❱❱ In a frying pan, combine the olive oil, garlic, onion, lime juice, salt, and pepper. Stir well and heat over medium-high heat until it starts simmering, 1 to 2 minutes. Pour over the vegetables and gently toss. Adjust the seasoning and serve immediately.

SWEET POTATO, GREEN PLANTAIN & SCALLION LATKES

T hese latkes are everything a latke should be—moist and crisp, with lots of flavor from the scallions, parsley, and pesto topping. They also make a great side to grilled steak or chicken.

» Preheat the oven to 200°F. Line a baking sheet with several layers of paper towels.

» Place the plantain in a pot and cover with salted water. Bring to a boil and cook until the plantain is very soft and easily pierced with a fork, 15 to 20 minutes. Drain well and transfer to a large bowl. Mash with a fork until almost smooth. Let cool.

» Add the shredded sweet potato, egg, scallions, and parsley. Mix well and season with salt and pepper. Shape into 3-inch patties.

» In a nonstick frying pan, heat the oil over medium heat. Place a few patties at a time in the pan and fry until golden brown and crisp, 5 to 6 minutes on each side. Place the cooked patties on the prepared sheet pan and keep warm in the oven while cooking the remaining patties. Serve hot with the pesto.

- 1 pound green plantains, peeled and cut into chunks
- 1 sweet potato, peeled and shredded or coarsely grated
- 1 large egg, lightly beaten
- 2 scallions, thinly sliced
- 1 tablespoon finely chopped fresh parsley
- 2 teaspoons fine sea salt
- 1 teaspoon freshly ground black pepper
- 2 teaspoons vegetable oil
- Cassava Leaves Pesto (page 141), for serving

SAINT-LOUIS, A COLONIAL CITY WHERE LAND AND WATER MEET

"Thiebou jenn Penda Mbaye!" goes the chorus of a popular song in Senegal. Penda Mbaye is a fabled Saint-Louis woman whose name has become synonymous with delicious *thiebou jenn*. In fact, her *thiebou jenn* was reputed to be so good that a classic *sabar* song has been dedicated to it.

Aside from being the first colonial capital, Saint-Louis is, above all, Senegal's gastronomic capital. After all, this is the place where our national dish originated. The women here are notorious for their "seasoned hands" (*saf loxo* in Wolof, meaning "great cook") and their elegance. Since the time of the *signares* (from the Portuguese *senhoras* or "ladies"), Saint-Louis women have stayed true to that reputation.

It is said that the best time to glimpse their charms is between the late-afternoon Muslim prayer and sunset, a time that's known in Wolof as *Takkussan Ndar* or "Saint-Louis's Sunset." It's a tradition that dates from the colonial era: come *takkussan*, Saint-Louis women dress to kill (as they say) in their colorful gowns and matching gold jewelry, exhaling the voluptuous fragrance of *thiou-ray*, the sensual local incense. Slowly parading the arteries of the island, they converge on Place Faidherbe, the main square on the island for social time, in style.

Saint-Louis, declared a UNESCO World Heritage Site in 2000, is also where my uncle and namesake, Mgr. Pierre Sagna, is buried. He was the first Senegalese bishop of Saint-Louis and as such, his tomb is placed right by the altar inside the Saint-Louis Cathedral, the oldest in West Africa. Clearly, I have a particular affinity for this food city; it's always a double pilgrimage whenever I visit Saint-Louis.

Walking around the old city feels like time traveling, as the city seems frozen in the colonial era. This feeling is even stronger on Ndar, or "The Island," as the old-city neighborhood is commonly called. In 1659, Ndar was developed and named after King Louis XIV, making Saint-Louis the first permanent French settlement in Senegal. It has since kept the colonial architectural style: narrow streets are lined by colorful houses with balconies and inner courtyards reminiscent of New Orleans and Havana. Many of the colonial houses are in need of restoration, but some historical sites and hotels are still in excellent condition. Among them is Jamm, which translates to "peace" in Wolof. It's an appropriate name for this stunningly restored home, owned by my friend Yves Lamour and arguably one of the best bed and breakfasts on the island.

If one monument could truly symbolize Saint-Louis, it would be Pont Faidherbe, a bridge that connects the island to the Sor quarter on the mainland. The bridge, inaugurated on Bastille Day in 1897, was recently renovated. An enduring myth claims that it was built by Gustave Eiffel who built the Eiffel Tower (in reality, he lost the bidding contract for its construction).

My favorite spot in Sor, where mostly the working class and fishermen live, is Hôtel Dior. The hotel is named after its owner, a gorgeous and gracious hostess who tastefully decorated each of the comfortable bungalows built around a swimming pool facing the Langue de Barbarie, the miles-long thin sandy beach separating the Atlantic and the Senegal River.

CASSAVA LEAVES PESTO

Cassava leaves can be found in the frozen food section of West African markets. I've also found them in Chinatown, usually in stores that have Southeast Asian or Filipino products.

For the pesto, the cassava leaves can be substituted with most greens; kale or sweet potato greens work especially well and keep the nutrition factor high. Serve it spread on crostini or in a sandwich, tossed with grains for a salad (page 163), or even in a simple pasta dish.

2 cups packed chopped cassava leaves, sweet potato leaves, or kale

⅓ cup raw cashew nuts, coarsely chopped

3 garlic cloves, minced

Juice of 1 lemon

¼ cup red palm oil or vegetable oil

¼ cup vegetable oil

Fine sea salt and freshly ground black pepper

⟩⟩ Bring a pot of salted water to a boil. Add the cassava leaves and cook for only a few seconds. Drain the leaves, then cool under cold running water. Squeeze out the excess water with your hands.

⟩⟩ Combine the cassava leaves with the cashews in a mortar and mix well with the pestle. Add the garlic and pound until smooth. Add the lemon juice and mix again.

Slowly add the red palm oil and vegetable oil in a slow stream and keep pounding until well combined. Season with salt and pepper to taste.

⟩⟩ Alternatively, this can be done by pulsing the cassava leaves, cashews, garlic, and lemon juice in a food processor. Stream in the oils, making sure to scrape down the sides of the bowl as you go.

ONION YASSA SOUP

2 tablespoons vegetable oil

5 to 6 cups thinly sliced yellow onions

2 dried bay leaves

Juice of 5 limes

5 cups chicken or vegetable stock

Fine sea salt and freshly ground black pepper

2 red bell peppers, roasted (see Note)

2 yellow bell peppers, roasted (see Note)

Croutons or puffed rice (optional), for serving

Yassa chicken, a delicious dish of caramelized onions, lime, and chicken, is one of Senegal's most famous dishes. Inspired by that dish, this soup requires just a few humble ingredients, but the flavors are complex and deep. The sweetness released from the slowly cooked onions combines with the smokiness of roasted peppers and the acidity of lime to create all the comforting traditional *yassa* flavors in one soup pot.

» In a large pot, warm the oil over medium heat. Add the onions and stir until they are evenly coated. Tightly cover with a lid and cook for about 20 minutes or until the onions are tender. Raise the heat and allow the onions on the bottom of the pot to slightly color before stirring with a wooden spoon. Tightly cover once again, reduce the heat, and repeat the process. When all the onions have evenly turned light brown, add the bay leaves, the juice of 4 of the limes, and the stock and season with 1 teaspoon salt and ½ teaspoon pepper. Bring to a boil, then reduce the heat and simmer for about 30 minutes.

» Cut the roasted peppers into ½-inch pieces. Add the peppers and the remaining lime juice to the pot. Remove the bay leaves and serve hot. Garnish with croutons or puffed rice, if you like.

NOTE: *There are several methods to roast bell peppers, but I prefer the one using an open flame. It gives a firmer and smokier pepper, which is great for texture and flavor.*

To roast the peppers, grill the peppers over the open flame of a gas stove or under a broiler using a pair of tongs to turn the peppers around to char all the sides. When the peppers are charred on all sides, immediately put them in a heatproof bowl and tightly cover with plastic wrap. This creates steam that will help the skin come off.

After about 30 minutes, remove the plastic wrap and gently peel the peppers; the skin should easily slip off. Do not rinse off the bits of charred skin that may cling to the pepper after peeling because you will lose most of the smoky flavor. Slice open the peppers and remove and discard the stem, seeds, and inner membrane. If using later, you can keep them sliced or whole. Roasted peppers can be stored in the refrigerator in an airtight container for up to 4 days.

GINGER BUTTERNUT SQUASH SOUP

SERVES
6

Although butternut squash is said to have originated in the Americas, its African counterpart, the calabash gourd (*Lagenaria siceraria*), may very well be the oldest plant domesticated by humans. From time immemorial, Africans have had a love affair with gourds, so we easily welcomed and embraced the new gourd, butternut squash. The leaves, flesh, and seeds of gourds are eaten in a variety of stews, soups, and sauces; the shells are dried and turned into kitchen bowls or gorgeous bottles that may be used to carry fresh milk or palm wine. Here, I roast and purée the squash into a spicy, tangy soup with ginger and red palm oil, and top it with a few of my favorite Senegalese touches.

4 cups peeled, seeded, and cubed butternut squash

¼ cup red palm oil or vegetable oil

3 onions, thinly sliced

1 tablespoon peeled, chopped fresh ginger

6 cups vegetable stock or water

1 teaspoon cayenne pepper

Juice of 1 lemon

Salt

OPTIONAL TOPPINGS

3 tablespoons toasted pumpkin seeds

Moringa Mint Salt (page 219)

Rof Gremolata (page 243)

2 tablespoons red palm oil

》 Preheat the oven to 400°F.

》 In a large bowl, toss the squash cubes with 2 tablespoons oil to coat well. Spread in a single layer on a rimmed baking sheet. Roast until soft and caramelized, 30 to 40 minutes, turning over the squash with a spatula about halfway through. Remove from the oven.

》 In a large pot, heat the remaining 2 tablespoons oil over medium heat. Add the onions and ginger and cook, stirring occasionally, for about 10 minutes, until the onions are soft.

》 Add the vegetable stock and roasted squash. Bring to a boil, reduce the heat, and simmer for 10 to 15 minutes.

》 Working in batches, transfer the soup to a blender, filling it up no higher than halfway. Blend the soup until very smooth. (Make sure to firmly hold down the lid or else the trapped steam may cause the soup to explode.) Alternatively, blend the soup in the pot with an immersion blender. If you'd like your soup extra smooth, strain through a fine-mesh sieve.

》 Stir in the cayenne and lemon juice and season with salt to taste. Serve hot with any one or a combination of the suggested toppings.

THE MIRACLE TREE

Moringa, or the "miracle tree" as it is sometimes called, grows abundantly in Senegal. It is such a nutritional powerhouse that its other name is *nevedaye*, as in "never die." For centuries, all parts of the *moringa* tree have been used for medicinal purposes. The crushed seeds are used for water purification and, with their high oil content, make great cooking oil and are even used as a spice. In Senegal, the leaves are most commonly eaten either fresh or dried and ground into a powder. *Moringa* leaves can be eaten raw in salads, sautéed, or cooked down into any number of stews and soups. In powder form, it can be sprinkled over a dish or easily stirred into stews, soups, and rice dishes.

SENEGALESE SPOTLIGHT:

Sunu Harvest

In Senegal, I got to know Pape Mayelad, one of the founders of Sunu Harvest, a company that creates products from natural tropical superfoods, particularly *moringa* and baobab. Beyond its product lines, in an effort to help fight malnutrition, Sunu Harvest also aims to educate local communities on the best ways to consume these products while retaining their nutritional value. In addition, their goals include creating jobs globally and developing a sustainable model of agricultural practice in Africa with direct social and economic benefits to rural communities. The leaves they use are sourced in collaboration with the rural community of Djilakh, where Sunu Harvest has a farm that is in the very expensive process of being certified organic.

Pape told me that "in Africa, women, kids, and senior citizens are usually deprived of balanced nutritional food. Using these products the right way will provide the necessary supplement to complete a healthy diet." He believes that a good way to retain the nutritional value of *moringa* leaves is to use them in dried form, sprinkled over your food, rather than cooking them.

Like many advocates of local Senegalese ingredients, Pape's goal is for moringa and plants like it "to play a very strong part in the global supply food chain," and quality is key. "We have strong plants that can be made into miraculous products, but we need to standardize their production for consistent quality and large volumes."

MORINGA & KALE SUPERGREENS SOUP

Using some of Senegal's favorite supergreens, this soup is as healthy as it is beautiful with its bright green color. Fresh *moringa* is preferred, but it is still quite potent in its powdered form and works great with the kale.

⊙

» Heat the olive oil in a large pot over medium-high heat. Add the onion, ginger, and garlic and cook, stirring constantly, for 2 to 3 minutes, until soft but not browned. Add the yuca and stock and bring to a boil. Reduce the heat to a simmer and cook gently for 10 to 15 minutes, until the yuca is soft.

» Add the moringa and about two-thirds of the kale. Season with 1 tablespoon salt and 1 teaspoon pepper and simmer for 5 to 10 minutes, until the kale softens.

» Working in batches, transfer the soup to a blender along with the remaining one-third of the kale, the lime juice, and cilantro, filling it up no higher than halfway. Blend the soup until very smooth. (Make sure to firmly hold down the lid or else the trapped steam may cause the soup to explode.) Alternatively, blend the soup in the pot with an immersion blender. Season with salt and pepper to taste. Add a little more stock or water if you want your soup less thick.

» Serve hot with a few dots of red palm oil and a tiny pinch of hibiscus-chile salt, if desired.

2 tablespoons olive oil or light vegetable oil

1 yellow onion, coarsely chopped

1 tablespoon peeled, chopped fresh ginger

1 tablespoon chopped garlic

3 cups peeled, coarsely chopped yuca

2 quarts vegetable stock or water

2 cups packed moringa leaves or fresh spinach or 5 tablespoons moringa powder

1 bunch kale, trimmed and coarsely chopped

Salt and freshly ground black pepper

Juice of 2 limes

2 tablespoons chopped fresh cilantro

2 tablespoons red palm oil (optional)

Hibiscus-Chile Salt (page 219; optional)

GRAINS

BASIC FONIO

1 cup uncooked fonio
Salt

This healthy, gluten-free grain can be used as a side in the same way you would use rice, couscous, or quinoa. These are two basic methods for steaming *fonio*. You can cook it in a steamer basket (the traditional way) or just in a pot on the stove. I've also had success cooking it in the rice cooker, if you have one (keep the ratio of fonio to water 1:1). You can always add a little bit of butter or oil to the fonio while cooking to keep the grains more separated, if you'd like. If you can't find fonio, quinoa would make a good substitute when it is called for throughout the book.

◉

» In a large bowl, wash the fonio grains by submerging in warm water, swishing the grains around with your fingers, then pouring out and replacing the water several times until it runs clear. Drain well.

» **Using a steamer:** Place the fonio in the top of a steamer basket lined with damp cheesecloth. Set over simmering salted water, cover, and steam for about 15 minutes. Remove from the heat and fluff with a fork. Drizzle a few tablespoons of salted water over the fonio and steam again until the grains are completely tender, another 5 to 10 minutes. Fluff with a fork and serve.

» **Without a steamer:** Bring 1 cup of water to a boil in a medium pot. Stir in the cleaned raw fonio and 1 tablespoon of salt, cover tightly with the lid, and turn the heat to low. Cook for about 2 minutes, until the water is just absorbed. Turn off the heat and gently fluff with a fork, making sure you fluff the bottom where it's wetter. Cover again for another 5 to 10 minutes, until tender.

SLOW-COOKED
LAMB FONIO TABOULEH

4

Inspired by North African tabouleh, this is a delicious combination full of flavors and colors. The lamb is so tender when shredded that it seems to melt into the *fonio*. The salad is bright and fresh with cucumber and herbs, and is also a great way to use up leftover lamb *dibi* (see page 228).

》 Preheat the oven to 225°F.

》 **To prepare the lamb:** In a large oven-safe pot, such as a Dutch oven, combine the lamb shanks, onion, garlic, bay leaves, thyme, and water. Bring to a boil, cover, and transfer to the oven. Cook for 5 hours, or until the lamb is very tender.

》 Remove from the oven and let the lamb cool in the liquid until it is easy to handle.

》 Remove the lamb from the cooking liquid and set aside. Strain the cooking liquid into a small pot and discard the solids. Over high heat, reduce the liquid by half. Set aside to cool and skim and discard the fat that rises to the top.

》 While the cooking liquid is reducing, shred the lamb and discard the bones, fat, and membranes. Season the lamb with salt and pepper to taste.

》 **To prepare the vinaigrette:** In a small bowl, combine ½ cup of the reduced cooking liquid, the lemon juice, mustard, salt, and pepper and whisk to dissolve the salt. Slowly pour in the oil, whisking constantly to emulsify.

》 **To prepare the tabouleh:** Place the fonio in a large bowl and add the shredded lamb, parsley, mint, cucumber, tomatoes, and microgreens. Toss well and generously fold in the vinaigrette to taste. (You may have some left over.) Top with the olives (if using). Serve immediately.

LAMB
- 2 lamb shanks (about 1¼ pounds each)
- 1 yellow onion, coarsely chopped
- 2 garlic cloves, unpeeled, crushed with the side of a knife
- 2 dried bay leaves
- 2 sprigs thyme
- 2 quarts water
- Salt and freshly ground black pepper

VINAIGRETTE
- Juice of 2 lemons
- 1 teaspoon Dijon mustard
- 1 teaspoon salt
- ½ teaspoon freshly ground black pepper
- 1 cup olive oil

TABOULEH
- 2 cups cooked fonio (page 150) or quinoa
- 1 bunch parsley, leaves finely chopped
- 1 bunch mint, leaves finely chopped
- 1 Kirby cucumber, peeled and diced
- 1 cup grape tomatoes, halved
- 1 cup microgreens or baby arugula
- ½ cup small green olives, pitted (optional)

GRAINS **153**

ANCIENT GRAIN, FORGOTTEN FONIO

"*Fonio* never embarrasses the cook." —BAMBARA PROVERB

onio is truly a West African treasure, a secret that should be shared with the world. A very small, seed-like type of millet, it is one of the most nutritious grains you can find. Although it has been cultivated in West Africa for thousands of years, Africa's oldest grain remains relatively unknown to the world and is neglected by Africans themselves who have turned to imported rice. Indeed, *fonio* was once a major food cultivated across the savannas all the way to ancient Egypt. Considered a delicacy, in some places it is reserved for only chiefs and royalty. *Fonio* has been largely neglected by the scientific community despite its importance as a major part of the diet of close to 4 million people in the regions of Mali, Guinea, Burkina Faso, and Nigeria. There is huge potential for its inclusion in diets all over the world, generating income for local African producers.

This gluten-free supergrain, packed with protein, vitamins, and minerals, is not only extremely healthy for you, it's also one of the best-tasting cereal grains. When steamed, *fonio* is fluffy and a little nutty, quite similar to couscous or quinoa. According to studies published in the *Journal of Food Science and Technology*, as opposed to most major grains, *fonio* has an abundance of cystine and methionine, two amino acids that are very important in nerve transmission and proper heart function. *Fonio* has a low glycemic index, is high in fiber and other phytonutrients, and is gluten-free, making it especially ideal for those with celiac disease or diabetes.

In Senegal, *fonio* is cultivated in Casamance and the southeastern regions of Tambacounda and Kedougou. Highly adaptable in difficult growing conditions and able to thrive in poor soil, *fonio* is also drought resistant and one of the fastest-maturing grains. *Fonio*'s versatility makes it one of my favorite grains. It can be used as a nutritious substitute for rice and couscous, made into a salad, cooked down to porridge, and even ground into flour for baking. As a salad with grilled vegetables, or with slow-cooked lamb for one-dish comfort (page 228), served sushi-style (page 173), or even combined with buckwheat to make soba-like noodles, "*fonio* never embarrasses the cook" as the famous Bambara saying goes.

SENEGALESE SPOTLIGHT:

Mrs. Aya Ndiaye, Fonio Queen

In Senegal, *fonio* is mostly consumed in the southern regions of Casamance, Tambacounda, and Kedougou where it is traditionally grown. Many Dakar urbanites may have never heard of *fonio*. To these city people, some of Senegal's best-tasting and healthiest grains like millet or *fonio* are considered stuff for backward country people.

However, in Kedougou, where Mrs. Aya Ndiaye lives, *fonio* is king. It is still seen as the exquisite treat that was served to royalty and special guests from time immemorial.

Mrs. Aya Ndiaye is one of the twenty-five founding members of a women-run cooperative called the Koba Club (a koba is an antelope found from Senegal to Sudan; it is also the animal totem of the locality). In what started as a hand-dyed batik fabric project almost thirty years ago, Mrs. Aya and her visionary partners saw the growing interest in local food transformation. Soon enough, processing local food products like baobab fruit juice, shea butter, red palm oil, and *fonio* quickly took over.

To Mrs. Aya, *fonio* has so much potential in the world market. "It's a unique product that requires no fertilizers. It strives in poor soil, and it matures really fast. In addition, *fonio* has always been considered the food for kings and princes."

Mrs. Aya is a little woman with a permanent shy smile. But behind that seeming gentleness is a powerful leader who was able to motivate her coworkers into producing the best-processed *fonio* in town. The market was local at first, but she kept at it. She had high standards and didn't want anything less than perfectly cleaned *fonio*. This meant triple-washing the hulled grains to make sure no sand got into the package.

Because *fonio* is a food that's recommended to those with a type of diabetes common in Senegal, Mrs. Aya started to receive invitations from nutritionists to teach its preparation at different hospitals around the country. Soon she was doing *fonio* tasting sessions at the University of Dakar.

Fonio gave Mrs. Aya and the Koba Club national recognition. In 2012, she was awarded a medal from the president of Senegal recognizing her work. She's received grants and support from different NGOs including the United States African Development Foundation (USADF), which helped to improve the Koba Club's means of processing. They also partnered with a branch of USAID called Wula Nafaa. "It's a program that focuses on export-oriented activities to increase household and enterprise revenues, predominately in the agriculture and natural resource sectors. They trained us and organized programs in hospitals and universities around the country where we would have cooking demos and tastings of *fonio* products," she told me.

The Koba Club's original founding members are now training their daughters to take over the cooperative. The harvest is collected in a big house that serves as a processing facility. It is first stored in large jute bags before it is carefully sifted. An all-woman crew wearing hairnets and flowery dresses does all the work.

After the sifting, the *fonio* is mechanically hulled in the processor, then sifted once again and washed several times in large calabashes until the water runs clear. The grains, still wet from washing, are then steamed over a giant pot of boiling water. Once steamed, the grains are spread on sheet pans and covered with mosquito net screens before being taken into the solar grain-drying unit. After drying, they are returned to the processor to separate the clumps that may have formed from the humidity. Finally, the processed grains are packaged and vacuum-sealed in 1-kilogram plastic bags with a Koba logo printed on it.

Mrs. Aya told me that the Koba Club has changed lives. "Before, it was a struggle to sell fifty kilos, but since we are established, we are selling out every season and are now able to prefinance farmers."

The *fonio* processor was invented in 1996 by Sanoussi Diakite, a Senegalese mechanical engineer. Prior to its invention, *fonio's* tiny grains were hand processed with a traditional mortar and pestle, which took a very long time. Mr. Diakite's machine was revolutionary to processors such as the Koba Club, and he received a Rolex Award for Enterprise for his invention in 1996.

MANGO FONIO SALAD

Juice of 2 lemons

1 teaspoon salt

½ teaspoon freshly ground
black pepper

1 cup olive oil

2 cups cooked fonio (page
150) or quinoa

1 bunch parsley, leaves finely
chopped

1 bunch mint, leaves finely
chopped

1 ripe mango, peeled, pitted,
and diced

½ red onion, finely chopped

1 cup red and yellow grape
tomatoes, halved

1 small cucumber, seeded and
diced

½ cup Spiced Cashews (page
87; optional)

B ursting with fresh herbs, lemon, and mango, and super easy to throw
together, this healthy grain salad would make a great addition to picnics
or potlucks as a side for grilled fish or meat or as a vegetarian main. Think
of this salad as a template to which you can add any number of your seasonal
produce favorites.

◉

» In a small bowl, combine the lemon juice with the salt and pepper. Slowly pour in the oil, whisking to emulsify.

» Place the fonio in a large bowl and add the parsley, mint, mango, onion, tomatoes, and cucumber. Toss well and generously fold in the vinaigrette to taste. (You may have some left over.) Top with the spiced cashews (if using) and serve immediately.

SPRING VEGETABLE FONIO PILAF

- 2 tablespoons red palm oil or olive oil
- 1 shallot, thinly sliced
- 1 garlic clove, minced
- 1 large carrot, peeled and diced
- ½ cup vegetable stock or chicken stock
- ½ pound baby zucchini, trimmed
- ½ pound asparagus, trimmed and cut into ½-inch lengths
- ¼ cup fresh or frozen green peas
- 2 cups cooked fonio (page 150) or quinoa
- 2 scallions, thinly sliced
- Salt and freshly ground black pepper

T his simple *fonio* pilaf makes the perfect side dish for the Lamb Shank Mafé (page 242) or any other main dish that needs a healthy grain to sop up its sauce. I use spring vegetables in this version, but feel free to adapt to whatever is in season.

» Heat the oil in a saucepan over medium-high heat. Add the shallot and cook until soft but not brown. Add the garlic and carrot and cook for another 3 minutes, until the garlic is fragrant. Add the stock and simmer, covered, until the carrot is tender, about 10 minutes.

» Cut the zucchini in half lengthwise, then into ½-inch pieces. Add the asparagus and zucchini to the pot and cook 5 minutes, until tender. Add the peas and cook for about 1 minute more. Fold in the fonio and scallions. Season with salt and pepper to taste. Serve hot or at room temperature.

CASSAVA PESTO MILLET SALAD

Whole grain millet and a flavor- and nutrient-packed pesto team up for this healthy, filling salad that couldn't be easier to prepare.

◎

» Wash the millet several times in a bowl until the water runs clear. Drain well. Rub the oil through the grains with your fingers. Place the millet in the top of a steamer basket lined with cheesecloth. Set over salted boiling water, cover, and steam for about 15 minutes or until tender and cooked through.

» Place the cooked millet in a wide bowl, cover with a clean kitchen towel, and let cool.

» Gently fold in the pesto and season with salt and pepper to taste. Top with the cashew nuts and serve immediately.

2 cups millet couscous (see Note)

¼ cup vegetable oil

1 cup Cassava Leaves Pesto (page 141)

Salt and freshly ground black pepper

½ cup roasted unsalted cashew nuts, coarsely chopped

NOTE: *If you can't find millet couscous, use regular hulled millet instead and follow the cooking directions on the package. I like to add a little butter or oil while cooking to prevent sticking. Quinoa also makes a good substitute.*

VEGETARIAN JOLLOF RICE

SERVES
4 TO 6

Jollof rice, one of the most popular and best-known dishes throughout West Africa, has many countries claiming it as their own. I can proudly, and correctly, say that the dish has Wolof origins, as Jollof is the name of an ancient Wolof kingdom in Senegal. From Senegal, the dish spread and evolved throughout West Africa, inspiring fierce regional preferences. At its simplest, jollof is a tomato-based rice dish, but depending on the region or even the household, the dish can incorporate different meats, seafood, vegetables, and spices. In Senegal, jollof serves as the base of the popular *thiebou jenn*. This is my vegetarian version, which works perfectly as a side dish or as a main rounded out with a few other dishes. If you have any rice left over, be sure to try my Herb-Stuffed Jollof Croquettes (page 111).

3 tablespoons vegetable oil

½ yellow onion, finely chopped

1 red bell pepper, thinly sliced

2 carrots, peeled and diced

3 plum tomatoes, chopped

2 cups tomato paste

¼ cup water

3 cups vegetable stock

1 dried bay leaf

Salt and freshly ground black pepper

2 cups basmati rice

1 cup fresh or frozen green peas, thawed

» In a large, heavy pot, such as a Dutch oven, heat the oil over medium-high heat. Add the onion, bell pepper, carrots, tomatoes, tomato paste, and water. Reduce the heat to low and slowly cook, stirring frequently with a wooden spoon to prevent scorching, about 15 minutes or until the oil starts to separate from the liquid and rises to the surface. Add the stock and bay leaf and season with salt and pepper. Bring to a boil, reduce the heat, and simmer for another 10 minutes, until well combined.

» Meanwhile, thoroughly wash the rice under running water until the water runs clear. Drain well.

» Add the rice to the vegetables and stir with a wooden spoon. Season again with salt and pepper. Bring the pot to a boil, then reduce to a simmer. Cover the pot with a tightly fitting lid and cook undisturbed for an additional 20 minutes or until the rice is fully cooked and tender. Add the peas and gently fold the rice to fluff it. Remove the bay leaf and serve hot.

CASAMANCE, THE GREEN HEART OF SENEGAL

The lush region of Casamance lies south of the Gambia River along the Casamance River. In contrast to the rest of Senegal, the tropical Casamance region has ample rainfall that supports a dense vegetation of mangroves and palm trees. The birthplace of my parents and their parents before them, Casamance is the land of rice paddies, palm wine, palm oil, honey, and fresh oysters. Casamance grows much of the food, rice, and cotton used by the rest of Senegal, making it the country's "bread basket." Its rich diversity, combined with the bountiful abundance of land and sea, make the perfect setting for great cuisine. Indeed, Casamance is magical.

Traveling to Casamance requires some degree of patience. Flying from Dakar, which takes a little less than an hour, would be ideal if only Senegal Airlines flights were more regular and predictable. Your other two travel options are either overnight by boat or, if you like an adventure, driving by road, the duration of which is often up to the moody customs officers at the border when crossing Gambia, and doubled by the lengthy wait for a ferry that's invariably delayed and congested.

The ship that provides the overnight boat ride from Dakar to Ziguinchor is named after our anticolonial hero-queen, Aline Sitoé. It leaves Dakar in the late afternoon to arrive early the next morning, greeted by dolphins that seem to be saying, "Welcome to Paradise!" Flamingos, manatees, monkeys, and many species of birds complete the idyllic scene.

Tucked between the former English colony Gambia and the former Portuguese colony Guinea-Bissau, and inhabited by a mix of ethnic groups including the Diola, Fulani, Mandinkas, and Manjack, Casamance has retained a distinct, rich cultural identity due to its relative isolation from the northern part of Senegal. Portuguese Creole is still widely spoken in the Casamance capital, Ziguinchor. Unlike the rest of Senegal, which is predominantly Muslim, many in Casamance are Christian, and some still practice animist traditions. Zig, the local nickname for the Casamance capital, is a crumbling city at the edge of the Casamance River. A typical Zig conversation can seamlessly go from Portuguese Creole to Wolof, French, Socé, or Diola. The diversity of cultures greatly contributes to making Casamance so special.

Whereas the rest of the country is a semidesert, here we have a landscape of tangled mangroves and thick tropical forests full of coconut, red palm fruit, and other types of palm trees. The majestic kapok tree, locally known as *bentenki*, is king here, rising even bigger and taller than the notorious savanna baobab. During the dry season between October and May, when the temperature drops to around 70°F, the region becomes a haven for bird migration, and pink flamingoes flock to the *bentenki's* tall branches to build their nests.

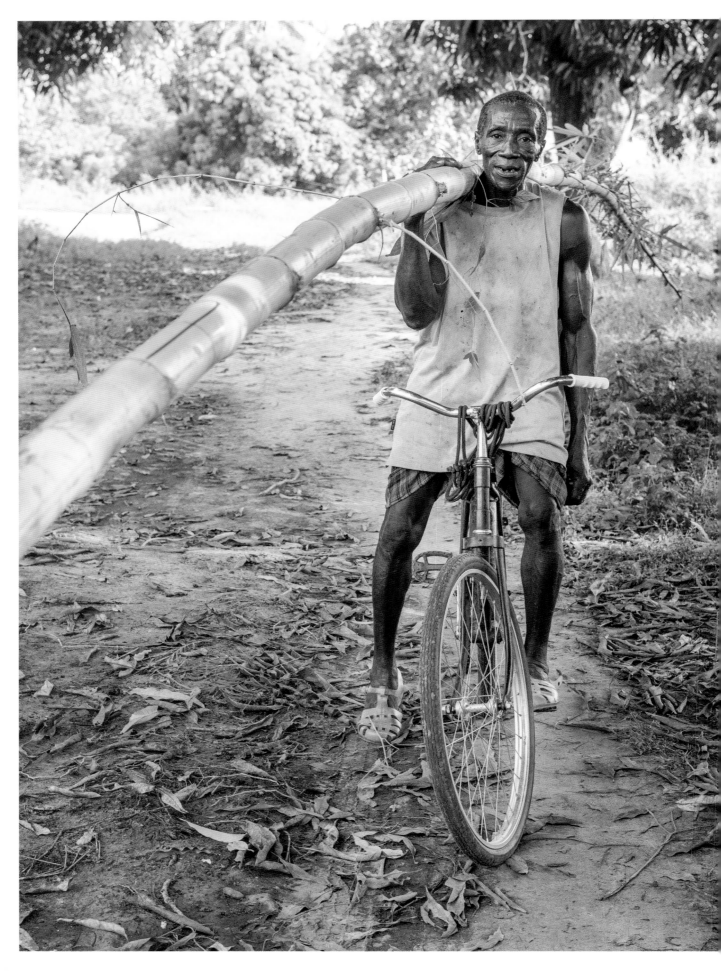

The dry season also means oysters abound. Oysters grow wild, clinging to the roots of mangrove trees, and are a big part of Casamance gastronomy, often served at wedding ceremonies, and eaten dried, boiled, or grilled. From July to September comes the abundant rainfall with temperatures rising to 90°F. That's when the palm wine is plentiful and the rice is harvested.

Casamance in its stunning splendor always feels like home. That feeling may be connected to the slower pace here—bicycling remains the favored way to get around—or perhaps it's in the comfort food, the citrusy grilled chicken *yassa* or the okra-and-seafood-laden *soupou kandja*, or maybe simply in the scent of warm rain. Regardless, it's a feeling that always lingers in the air.

Sandwiched between Gambia and Guinea, Casamance's isolation can also be frustrating. This physical alienation, combined with cultural differences, has led to an independence movement that started almost three decades ago. The low-level war has taken a toll on the region's economy, hurting tourism, which was one of the principal sources of employment. Miles of pristine beaches lined with palm trees, among the longest in West Africa, emptied. However, the situation has now greatly improved as ongoing negotiations between the separatist rebels and government are promising a lasting peace. Thankfully, investment is gradually returning to the region.

SWEET POTATO & GRILLED OKRA
FONIO SUSHI

The greatest thing about *fonio* is its versatility. I once brought some to my friend, Japanese soba master Chef Shuichi Kotani, who thought that *fonio* was reminiscent of its Japanese counterpart, buckwheat. (They are both ancient grains believed to be over 5,000 years old.) He ground the *fonio* into flour to make delicious *fonio* soba noodles and subsequently fell in love with it.

This recipe, in which I substitute sushi rice with whole grain, nutritional powerhouse *fonio*, is another nod to Japan. Light and healthy, I fill my nori-maki sushi with sweet potato and okra, some of my favorite Senegalese vegetables.

2 cups cooked fonio (page 150) or quinoa

¼ cup soy sauce

2 tablespoons red palm oil or vegetable oil

1 teaspoon lime juice

16 whole okra pods, trimmed (see Note)

1 cup roasted mashed sweet potato

4 sheets nori (seaweed)

1 large ripe mango, peeled, seeded, and cut into ½-inch-thick batons or Pickled Mango (page 86)

¼ cup thinly sliced scallions

NOTE: *Trim the narrow points of the okra so the pods are evenly thick in the rolls.*

» Preheat the grill or a grill pan to hot.

» With a small mortar and pestle, mash half of the cooked fonio into a paste. Combine with the rest of the fonio to make it sticky. Combine the soy sauce, oil, and lime juice in a small bowl. Stir 1 tablespoon into the fonio and set the rest aside for dipping later.

» Grill the okra, turning once, for 3 to 5 minutes, until lightly charred and tender. Set aside to cool.

» Lay a nori sheet on a sushi mat and evenly spread a thin layer of the fonio, leaving about 1 inch bare along the edge opposite you. Spread a few tablespoons of the mashed sweet potato along the closest edge to you. Line up a few okra, tip to tip, next to the sweet potato. Lay a few pieces of mango, tip to tip, next to the okra.

» Tightly roll up the sushi mat around the nori and the filling. Slightly wet the exposed end of the nori with water and seal. Repeat the process with the remaining nori sheets and filling.

» With a sharp knife, slice the rolls into small rounds. Serve immediately with the soy dipping sauce, topped with the scallions.

SACRED RICE

Rice is at the heart of the Diola community. Rituals such as weddings, funerals, and initiations all include a rice-connected custom. Confessions and prayers for rain at traditional shrines and sacrifices to win the favor of Emitai (the Diola supreme being) all involve rice. The Diolas' refusal to use sacred rice to pay the tax to support the French colonizers' war effort led to one of the most symbolic anticolonialist resistances and the subsequent deportation of Casamance hero Aline Sitoé.

Among the Diola people of Casamance, the cultivation of rice is a community affair. The whole operation is gender based. First, the women select the seeds that will be planted. Then when the rainy season arrives and it is time for planting, the men get together and in groups prepare the soil of every rice field in the community. While working the paddy fields, they often sing for motivation in a call-and-response pattern reminiscent of the blues. The Diola men use the *kajandu*, the long-handheld fulcrum shovel that has come to symbolize Diola men, to work the paddy fields. When harvest season comes, it's then the women's turn to get together to collect the rice. As they cut the blades of rice by hand with a sharp curved tool, they too sing and sometimes even break into dance.

Each Diola family has a barn for rice storage on their compound. In addition, there is a community barn in the village that's designated for the needy or the traveler because no one must ever go hungry or have to beg for food in Diola society. It is an established tradition that every family contributes a portion of their harvest for this communal "needy barn" that is accessible to everyone and is considered a positive sign of abundance. The rice stored in it can sometimes age for many years.

After all the pastoral work is done, the time comes to thank the ancestors for the bountiful harvest and the whole community goes into celebration mode. Communally cooked rice dishes washed down with palm wine and dancing of *Jambadong* or *Ekonkon* (traditional Mandinka and Diola dances, respectively) to the rhythm of frenetic drums mark the end of the harvest.

SENEGAL'S JOAN OF ARC

In the midst of a drought in Casamance, during World War II, a young handicapped Diola woman named Aline Sitoé Diatta received a revelation from Emitai, the supreme being in Diola mythology. She was instructed to introduce rituals and practices that would bring rain in abundance, and called upon the elders to share her revelations.

Among the instructions given, the Diola people were to return to an ancient ritual known as Huyaye, which allocates a day of rest for the rice paddies. Aline Sitoé insisted that they strictly grow and use the local rice, *Oryza glabberima*, for their religious rituals as it was the rice given to them by Emitai and carried the spiritual link to their ancestors. She argued that the imported broken rice that French colonial authorities flooded the market with had no spiritual value. Additionally, Emitai had ordered the Diola to oppose other French agricultural schemes, including their orders to grow cash crops such as peanuts, which were planted at the cost of the diversity of Casamance forests, risking symbolic Diola products such as palm oil, palm wine, herbal medicines, and the habitats of local game.

Preaching rebellion and independence from French authorities, her movement was widely followed, but after a fierce resistance, she was arrested by the French and deported to Timbuktu where she died of starvation. Aline Sitoé Diatta was a true visionary and a precursor to the Green Revolution.

EGGPLANT & PALM OIL RISOTTO

with SORREL-OKRA SAUCE

Ingredients

- 2 cups basmati rice, washed
- 5 tablespoons red palm oil or vegetable oil
- 2 medium Japanese eggplants, cut into ½-inch cubes
- 1 large yellow onion, chopped
- 2 garlic cloves, chopped
- Salt and freshly ground black pepper
- 2 cups full-fat coconut milk
- 1 cup vegetable stock or water
- 2 tablespoons Vietnamese or Thai fish sauce
- 1 tablespoon chopped fresh parsley
- 1 tablespoon chopped fresh cilantro
- Juice of 1 lime
- Baguedj (recipe follows), for serving

This dish reminds me of a meal I used to eat at my grandparents' house in Casamance: a simple *nyankatang* (plain cooked rice) with a *tambadjan* (dried bonito) steamed right in it and served with palm oil. Sometimes Grandma would bury a golf ball–sized *suul* (a fermented locust bean mixture) in the steaming rice, infusing the whole dish with a deep savory flavor. In this recipe, the fermented flavor comes from fish sauce. If you're vegetarian, you can leave the fish sauce out.

◉

» Soak the rice in water for 1 hour, up to overnight. Drain.

» In a skillet, heat 2 tablespoons of the oil over medium heat. Add the eggplant with half of the onion and garlic. Season with salt and pepper and stir frequently until the eggplant is soft. Remove from the heat.

» In a heavy pot, such as a Dutch oven, heat 2 tablespoons of the oil over medium heat. When the oil is hot, add the remaining onion and garlic. Cook, stirring frequently, until the onion is soft. Add the drained rice and stir well to coat. Add the coconut milk and stock and stir well. Bring to a boil, then reduce the heat to a simmer. Add the fish sauce. Cover tightly with a lid. Cook until the rice is tender and the liquid is absorbed, 15 to 20 minutes. Season with salt and pepper to taste.

» Fold in the remaining tablespoon of oil and the reserved eggplant. Top with the parsley, cilantro, and lime juice and serve hot with the baguedj on the side.

BAGUEDJ (SORREL-OKRA SAUCE)

Baguedj is a condiment for okra lovers. I love to serve it with fish and rice dishes such as *caldou* or white *thiebou jenn*. The acidity of the sorrel cuts particularly well through the unctuous okra in this beautiful, simple sauce.

Makes about 1 cup

4 or 5 okra pods, trimmed and coarsely chopped
2 bunches sorrel or 1 bunch spinach, coarsely chopped
1 Scotch bonnet pepper, seeded and chopped (optional)
1 tablespoon Vietnamese or Thai fish sauce
1 teaspoon freshly ground black pepper
1 tablespoon lemon juice (optional)

» In a small saucepan, cook the okra in boiling water until tender, about 5 minutes. Drain and set aside.

» In a separate pot, over medium heat, cook the sorrel with a few tablespoons of water, the Scotch bonnet (if using), and fish sauce until soft and wilted, about 5 minutes. Drain.

» In a food processor, purée the sorrel with the okra and black pepper. (If using spinach, add the lemon juice.) The mixture should be light; if too thick, add a little bit of water. Serve in a small bowl as a side to the eggplant risotto or any fish dish.

» Alternatively, you can also pound the cooked ingredients with a mortar and pestle or mix them together with a wooden spoon until the sauce holds. This method makes an airier sauce that looks almost like foam (the longer you mix, the airier it will get).

SPIRULINA RICE & COWPEAS

with SEARED SCALLOPS (DAKHIN)

RICE

2 cups jasmine rice

2 tablespoons peanut oil

1 yellow onion, chopped

2 tablespoons tomato paste, mixed with 2 tablespoons water

2 tablespoons unsweetened smooth peanut butter

½ cup dried cowpeas or black-eyed peas, soaked overnight and drained

1 quart vegetable or chicken stock

Fine sea salt and freshly ground black pepper

½ cup peanut flour (see page 68)

Pinch of nététou (see page 70) or 2 tablespoons Vietnamese or Thai fish sauce

1 tablespoon dried spirulina, diluted in ¼ cup water

SCALLOPS

16 sea scallops (diver scallops if possible), side muscle removed

¼ teaspoon fine sea salt

¼ teaspoon freshly ground black pepper

2 tablespoons peanut or olive oil

¼ cup roasted unsalted peanuts, coarsely chopped

2 tablespoons red palm oil (optional)

4 lime wedges

Dakhin is a traditional Senegalese risotto-like dish prepared with meat, rice, peanuts, and red cowpeas. In this version, I skip the meat and serve it with seared scallops instead. To give the dish a flavor, health, and color boost all in one, I've added a tablespoon of spirulina. Spirulina, an algae that grows naturally in Senegal, is considered a powerful superfood. It is a great source of protein, minerals, vitamins, beneficial pigments, and antioxidants. I use the powdered form, which is most readily available and found in health-food stores. If you've had spirulina in smoothies and other "healthy drinks," you might find the green flavor quite strong. But here I dilute it in water first, and the flavor is balanced by other bold ingredients, giving the dish a deep savory taste with just a hint of the sea.

» **To prepare the rice:** Wash the rice thoroughly, then soak for about 1 hour.

» In a large saucepan, heat the peanut oil over medium heat and cook half of the onion, stirring frequently, until soft, but not brown. Add the tomato paste–water mixture and cook for 3 to 5 minutes until darker red in color, stirring frequently with a wooden spoon to avoid scorching.

» Add the peanut butter, peas, and stock. Bring to a boil, then reduce the heat to a simmer. Using a wooden spoon, stir well to incorporate the peanut butter. Add the remaining onion and season with salt and pepper. Simmer for about 30 minutes, until the oil rises to the surface.

» Add the rice, peanut flour, and nététou. Stir well to combine. Cover the pot with a tightly fitting lid and bring back to a boil. Reduce the heat and simmer, covered, for about 20 minutes, until the rice is cooked. Remove from the heat and fold in the spirulina-water mixture.

» When the rice is almost done, prepare the scallops. Pat the scallops dry with a clean towel and season with the salt and pepper.

» Heat the peanut oil in a large nonstick frying pan over medium-high heat until very hot. Add half the scallops and sear until browned, about 2 minutes per side. Remove from the pan and set aside, keeping the scallops warm. Sear the remaining scallops.

» To serve, spoon the spirulina rice in the center of a warmed plate. Top each serving with seared scallops, the peanuts, and a drizzle of red palm oil. Serve hot with the lime wedges.

A SYSTEM OF RICE PRODUCTION, BROKEN

Africa produces more grains than any other continent. *Oryza glaberrima*, one of two principal varieties of rice that exist in the world, was born in West Africa. It is the same rice that was brought to the Americas through the slave trade along with the captives, experts in its cultivation. Those captives were taken to the Carolinas, among other places in the Americas. There, the new crop quickly became a boon to the economy, and was even nicknamed "Carolina Gold." Among the captives were many Diola men and women from the Casamance region of Senegal, where part of my family originates and rice is held sacred.

The story of how our native rice became immensely successful across the Atlantic and neglected at home is a case study. *Thiep* (meaning "rice" in Wolof) is what Ivorians jokingly call Senegalese people. We are big rice consumers indeed. Rice is eaten more than any other grain in Senegal, but alas, only 45 percent of rice consumption is sourced locally. In a country where more than 30 percent of the daily caloric intake comes from rice, this reliance on such a heavily-imported sustenance grain is alarming. According to research by the German Development Institute, "no other country in sub-Saharan Africa is so food-import-dependent, especially on one specific product: rice."

Although rice production in West Africa has doubled since 1985, consumption has increased at an even higher rate due to population growth, further intensifying our dependence on rice imports. However, rice wasn't always central to the staple diet in Senegal. During precolonial times, the main cereal was millet; rice production was for the most part limited to the confines of Casamance and its consumption elsewhere a luxury.

Senegal's dependence on rice and its struggle to become self-sufficient dates back to colonial times when the French imposed the cultivation of cash crops such as peanuts and cotton. The French heavily promoted the cultivation of peanuts in Senegal in order to produce peanut oil for European markets. We subsequently became one of the world's leading exporters, producing almost one-quarter of the world's peanuts in the early 1960s.

Since much of our farmland was now dedicated to cash crops, we began importing our subsistence crops. Indochina, whose rice production was also controlled by the French, conveniently became our supplier. The French imported cheap broken rice, which is considered an inferior, substandard product (the leftovers from rice processing) on the international market. Broken rice became the rice of choice in Senegalese households and, half a century since independence, that preference remains today, especially in urban areas. Embraced by the population, it became the favorite choice in the preparation of popular dishes such as *thiebou jenn*. According to the Food and Agriculture Organization of the United Nations (FAO), today more than 95 percent of the rice Senegal imports is broken rice, and we are in fact the largest market for the product worldwide, with rice coming from not only Thailand and Vietnam, but also India, Pakistan, and Brazil. Since urban markets represent 65 percent of Senegalese rice consumers, and 90 percent of the urban market buys imported broken rice, this preference is a key obstacle to shifting consumption to domestic rice.

The food crisis in 2008 was a harsh awakening for countries such as Senegal, showing how our large dependency on imported rice makes us incredibly vulnerable to the volatility in the international market. It was a key opportunity to turn to domestic rice, but the supply could not meet the demand. In response, the government invested heavily in initiatives for boosting domestic production. However, as the import prices for rice soared, the government temporarily eliminated tariffs and even subsidized imports to try to keep the prices low, which conflicted with the goals of their own domestic programs. What is at stake beyond the livelihoods of rice growers and those directly involved in the industry is the food security of an entire nation and the opportunity to alleviate poverty and bring economic growth.

Of course, achieving such self-sufficiency is no simple task. On the supply side, there needs to be a greater and more reliable marketable surplus. Right now, the supply chain is challenged by a number of issues including a lack of fertilizer and seed markets that function well, high transaction costs, and limited access to credit. Government programs have focused on increasing production, but they have largely ignored how to create a demand for local rice and bring it to market.

One of the biggest obstacles is the existing preference for broken rice and the perception that local rice is of low quality. The small informal mills that most harvesters use do not sort rice mechanically because it's a task that rural households are used to taking on themselves at home. Ungraded conventional rice found at market is also usually a mix of varieties, sometimes of differing quality. So the first challenge is to upgrade the quality of the rice by improving the processing, milling, and drying. Such upgrades to infrastructure will surely require private sector investments. Once there is a high-quality product that aligns with consumer preferences, there are the challenges of bringing it to market and creating demand and awareness through branding, marketing, and promotion.

A few years ago, there was an experimental auction that showed that consumers in Dakar and Saint-Louis were willing to pay a premium price for branded, local, high-quality rice. There is amazing potential, but we seem stuck in an unsustainable system that our so-called independence hasn't yet figured out a way to resolve. Meanwhile, our native and much more nutritious rice only barely survives thanks to its sacred place in Diola culture. *Oryza glaberrima*, aka the prized Carolina Gold across the Atlantic, patiently awaits the day that it will become "Senegal Gold."

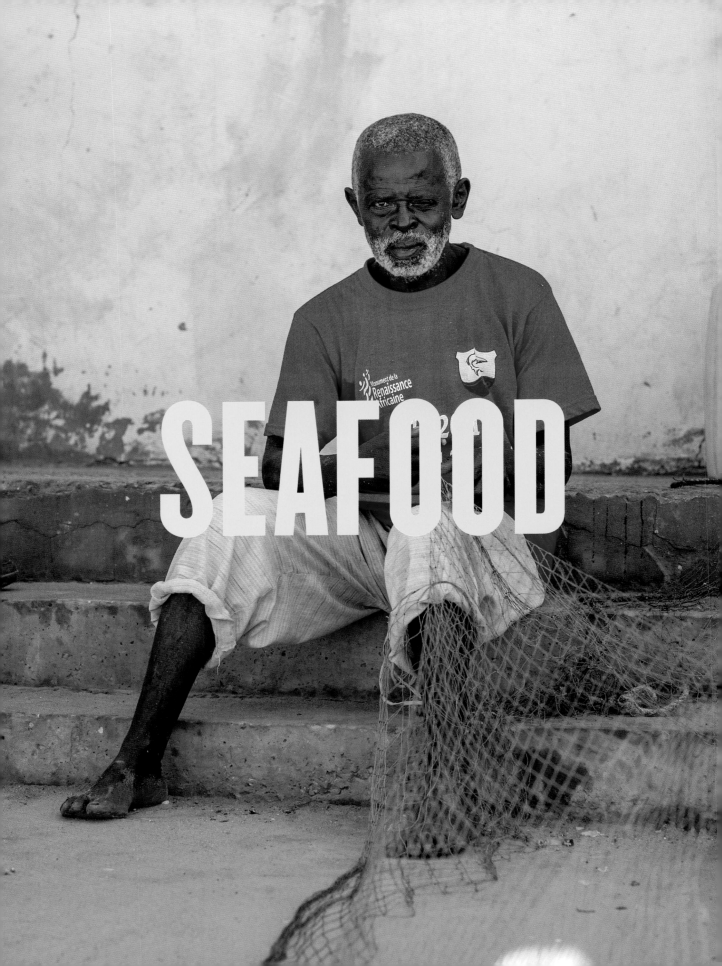

SEAFOOD

PAN-FRIED SEA BASS
(FIRIRE)

2 whole sea bass or red
  snapper (1½ to 2 pounds
  each), scaled and gutted

2 tablespoons Vietnamese or
  Thai fish sauce, or fine sea
  salt

Juice of 1 lime

1 teaspoon fine sea salt

1 teaspoon freshly ground
  black pepper

2 cups vegetable oil

1 cup all-purpose flour

Lime wedges, for serving

Tomato Onion Relish (page
  211), for serving

Firire, a corruption of the French *frire* ("to fry"), is what we call fried fish in Senegal. You can use fish fillets if you don't want to deal with fish bones, but in Senegal we like to eat with our hands, grabbing the head or the tail of the fish to better extract the hidden crispy bits of flesh that are missing from boneless fillets. Besides, I think that there is nothing more elegant than a whole fish served on a platter. Serve your *firire* with a side of Garlicky Mojo Root Vegetable Salad (page 136) or rice and you'll have a complete, satisfying meal.

◉

» Rinse the fish well and pat dry with paper towels. With a sharp knife, make two or three shallow slashes on each side of the fish.

» Place the fish in a shallow bowl or platter and sprinkle both sides with the fish sauce, lime juice, salt, and pepper. Allow the seasoning to penetrate the fish, 5 to 10 minutes.

» Line a baking sheet or platter with several layers of paper towels. In a large frying pan or cast-iron skillet, heat the oil over medium-high heat.

» Lightly dredge a fish in the flour and carefully place it in the hot oil; it should sizzle. Reduce the heat to medium and fry for 3 to 5 minutes, undisturbed. When the skin is crisp and has a deep golden color, carefully turn the fish onto its other side using a spatula. Cook undisturbed for another 3 to 5 minutes. Briefly drain the fried fish on the paper towels before transferring it to a serving dish. Keep warm, tented with aluminum foil. Repeat with the second fish.

» When both fish are cooked, serve hot with lime wedges and relish on the side.

SPORTS
LE SOLEIL - SAMEDI 4 ET DIMANCHE 5 MAI 20
JOSEPH MBOUNDOR SE
Le vétéran qui refus
d'aller à la retraite
BABOU SECK
MAMADOU GASKELL DIAMÉ :
Le jeune loup aux
dents acérées

SALMON-YUCA CROQUETTES

½ pound yuca, peeled and cut into 2-inch pieces

2 pounds boneless, skinless salmon fillet

1 yellow onion, finely chopped

1 tablespoon chopped fresh cilantro

2 teaspoons salt

1 teaspoon freshly ground black pepper

Vegetable oil, for frying

Spicy Tamarind Glaze (recipe follows), for serving

T his recipe, inspired by the traditional Senegalese *boulettes de poisson*, is a popular dish when I cater cocktail parties. In Senegal we wouldn't use salmon because it is not local; any firm-fleshed fish is a good option. I also substitute the soaked, stale baguette used as a binder in traditional *boulettes* with starchy yuca, which makes the dish gluten-free.

)) Place the yuca in a pot and cover with salted water. Bring to a boil, reduce the heat to medium, and cook until the yuca is very soft, about 20 minutes. Drain well and let cool until it is easy to handle. Remove and discard the string-like fibrous core and finely chop the yuca.

)) While the yuca is cooking, finely chop the salmon with a sharp chef's knife. Place the salmon in a large bowl.

)) Add the chopped yuca, onion, cilantro, salt, and pepper to the salmon and mix until well combined. Using your hands, shape into golf ball–size balls and set aside on a baking sheet or platter. When your hands get too sticky, rinse them under cold running water and continue shaping the balls until all the mixture is used.

)) Line another baking sheet or platter with several layers of paper towels. Pour oil into a large cast-iron skillet or other heavy, straight-sided pan to a depth of 1 inch, and heat to 365°F over medium-high heat. Fry the balls in batches until golden brown all over, turning with a slotted spoon. Remove with the slotted spoon and drain on the paper towels. Serve hot, drizzled with the tamarind glaze.

SPICY TAMARIND GLAZE

Makes 2 cups

½ cup tamarind pulp (about 6 ounces)
½ cup boiling water
¾ cup honey
¼ cup Vietnamese or Thai fish sauce
1 Scotch bonnet pepper, seeded and
    finely chopped
2 garlic cloves, minced

❱❱ Combine the tamarind pulp and boiling water in a heatproof bowl and let stand 10 minutes to soften. With a wooden spoon or your fingers, break the tamarind into small pieces. Let stand 5 minutes more. Pour the mixture through a coarse strainer set over another bowl and press with the spoon to squeeze the liquid from the seeds and fibers. Discard the seeds and fibers. Stir in the honey, fish sauce, Scotch bonnet, and garlic.

❱❱ The glaze can be made ahead and stored in the refrigerator in an airtight container for up to 1 month.

THE THEFT OF OUR WATERS

I stand with Ousmane on the sandy beach in Ouakam, surrounded by brightly painted pirogues, people exercising, a young boy washing a sheep in the water. We've returned from a trip with the fishermen whose catch was low, a common occurrence nowadays.

"I was born into a family of fishermen, as is almost everyone in the village of Ouakam. I grew up fishing. Artisanal fishing has been practiced in my family since the dawn of time. Although I went to elementary school, I've always been a fisherman. The sea is my universe," Ousmane says.

A local Lébou fisherman, Ousmane is seeing his livelihood threatened as the fish population of Senegal's coastal waters is being decimated. The consequences are far-reaching and escalating. This is a story, the story of many West Africans, not only in Senegal, that must be told.

In Ouakam, all activities are essentially devoted to fishing. At night, Ousmane and his brothers cast their nets; they return early the next morning to collect the harvest. Women are in charge of transforming the catch: smoking the fish, drying them, or selling them fresh at the market. Ouakam children learn to fish at a young age and oftentimes go fishing on the high seas in their colorful dugout boats for several days at a time. A huge part of the Senegalese population depends on fish as a major food source, and the fishing industry, both directly and indirectly, accounts for a large part of the country's employment.

The West African coast is one of the richest areas for fishing in the world, and the sea had been, until recent decades, wonderfully abundant. "There is a great diversity of fish and other seafood in our waters. Senegal's 'noble' fish were once abundant, but they are now increasingly rare: sole, mullet, captains, grouper, breams, and also octopus, prawns, lobsters, crabs. Here we are particularly fond of *thioff*, now an endangered species," explains Ousmane.

That bounty has attracted large foreign trawlers that practice illegal forms of fishing: fishing without permission from the authorities, using prohibited methods such as trawling with fine mesh that indiscriminately captures all kinds of fish and marine life, severely disturbing the ecosystem. It is estimated that it would take fifty traditional fishing pirogues a year to catch as much as one trawler does in a single day in these waters.

Ousmane tells me, "Unfortunately, the sea is not as abundant nowadays. We are victims of various abuses related to the exploitation of our waters. Russia, Korea, Spain, and other industrialized countries come into our territorial waters with large ships and scour the depths of our oceans, sometimes with the complicity of our government. We do not have the means to fight. Our fish population no longer has time to reproduce and they gradually disappear."

Poorly equipped Senegalese coast guards cannot control the entire coast, and there are corrupt authorities who sell illegal fishing licenses or take small bribes to turn a blind eye. Many ships offload their catches while at sea onto reefers (refrigerated vessels), avoiding the ports. This offshore laundering allows for inaccurate accounting of just how much fish is being caught and also hides the true origin of catches once they reach market.

According to reports by the United Nations' Africa Renewal program, West Africa loses around $1 billion USD worth of fish each year to illegal fishing, and *The Guardian* reports that catches are down 75 percent in the last ten years.

In addition to the illegal, unreported, and unregulated fishing by foreign trawlers, as the population of West Africa increases and as droughts continue to decimate crops throughout the region, more people than ever are coming to the coast to look for work in the fishing industry, adding even more pressure to the system. Coastal waters, which are reserved exclusively for local artisanal fishermen, are being depleted. Now the fishermen must go farther and farther out in dangerous waters unsuitable for their wooden boats to seek a good catch.

Much of this fish is bound for Europe, which has overfished its own waters and looks to other areas to sate its seafood demands. Ironically, overfishing in West Africa has led to a flood of migrants leaving West Africa to find work in Europe, where they are certainly not welcomed with open arms. Many risk their lives traveling up to 1,200 miles by sea to Spain's Canary Islands on the same wooden fishing boats powered only by a single outboard motor. Hundreds die or go missing in the perilous journey.

With the stability and food security of the area at stake, illegal fishing could ultimately lead to piracy and violence. Already comparisons are being made to the rise of pirates in Somalia, where similar complaints by Somali fishermen were heard in the 1990s at the beginnings of the civil war, as illegal fishing trawlers began to trespass in Somali waters. Driven to desperate measures, fishermen began to capture and ransom foreign trawlers and, later, commercial vessels.

To Ousmane, the ramifications of these illegal actions could be dire: "I am very worried. Unless there is a shift in consciousness and our politicians take concrete actions, this situation will only worsen. If we are not careful, we will be condemned to die of hunger. The survival of our community is directly connected to fishing."

The solution to such a huge problem is never simple. The social stability of West Africa is already fragile, and the widespread effects of illegal fishing could be disastrous. The first step is to raise awareness of the issues of illegal fishing; political activism in this regard is comparatively quite small. Coordination among governments throughout the region is vital—no one country can patrol these waters alone. Outdated fishing legislation must also be changed to better control legal fishing. In Senegal specifically, there are better contracts than in most other countries, but due to a lack of resources, they are not effectively enforced. To really face this problem head-on and with long-term goals, there must be prolonged commitments from African governments, outside aid, and security agencies to effect change.

GRILLED SARDINES

with MANGO SALSA (KOBO GRILLÉS)

Juice of 3 limes

1 Scotch bonnet pepper, finely chopped

2 teaspoons Dijon mustard

1 teaspoon fine sea salt

1 teaspoon freshly ground black pepper

2 garlic cloves, minced

3 pounds fresh sardines, scaled, gutted, rinsed and dried

2 red onions, thickly sliced

Mango Salsa (recipe follows), for serving

Kobo (or *yaboy*) is an affordable fish from the *Sardinella* genus found along the West African coast. They are usually a little bigger than the fresh sardines you'll see in the West, but basically have the same taste and bony structure. They are best eaten grilled over hot charcoal.

» In a bowl, whisk together the lime juice, Scotch bonnet, and mustard. Season with the salt and pepper and add the garlic. Pour the marinade over the sardines and onions in a shallow bowl or baking dish. Cover and refrigerate for 1 hour.

» Preheat the grill or a grill pan to hot. If the fish are very small, cover the grill grate with aluminum foil with holes punched through to keep the fish from falling through.

» Arrange the sardines and onions on the grill, and cook for about 3 minutes on each side. Serve hot with the mango salsa on the side.

MANGO SALSA

Makes about 2 cups

1 large ripe mango, peeled, pitted, and diced

1 red onion, thinly sliced

2 Scotch bonnet peppers, seeded and finely chopped

2 garlic cloves, minced

Juice of 2 limes

Grated zest of 1 lime

2 teaspoons freshly ground black pepper

2 teaspoons fine sea salt

2 tablespoons chopped fresh parsley

2 tablespoons chopped fresh basil

1 tablespoon chopped fresh cilantro

2 tablespoons red palm oil or vegetable oil

» Place all the ingredients in a bowl and gently fold until well combined. Serve as a side to grilled fish or mixed with baby greens as a salad. It can also be used as a marinade.

SMOKY TUNA TARTARE

with GREEN PLANTAIN CHIPS

Until recently, Senegalese waters were a haven for yellowfin tuna, which is now considered a "near threatened" (NT) species. Sadly, most of the fresh catch is destined to be boiled, deboned, and canned at the SNCDS (Société Nouvelle des Conserverie du Sénégal), the leading cannery in the country, which exports up to 25,000 tons of tuna a year to European markets. This treatment of what is among the best quality tuna is heartbreaking as all it needs is some fresh lime and seasoning.

I top this tartare with *kethiakh* (a traditional smoked and salted sardinelle) and pop *fonio*. The tartare has the clean, oceanic taste of the sea with a smoky umami flavor from the *kethiakh* and a bit of crunch from the pop *fonio*. It can be eaten as a snack or finger food over the plantain chips or molded on a plate as a more elegant first-course salad with a side of greens simply drizzled with oil. No matter how you serve it, remember to always use the freshest, highest-quality tuna when making a tartare.

1 pound sushi-grade tuna

¼ cup peanut oil or other light vegetable oil

2 teaspoons peeled, grated fresh ginger

2 tablespoons finely chopped fresh cilantro

1 tablespoon finely chopped scallion

1 tablespoon lime juice

1 teaspoon tamarind paste

½ teaspoon cayenne pepper

Fine sea salt and freshly ground black pepper

1 teaspoon smoked sardinelle (*kethiakh*; see Note)

Pop Fonio (page 120)

Green Plantain Chips (recipe follows)

NOTE: *If you cannot find* kethiakh, *smoked mackerel can be used, but it won't have quite the same smoky flavor.*

» Using a sharp knife, cut the tuna into small cubes. Combine the tuna with the oil, ginger, cilantro, scallion, lime juice, tamarind, and cayenne. Season with salt and pepper to taste.

» Top with the sardinelle and pop fonio. Serve immediately with the plantain chips.

GREEN PLANTAIN CHIPS

Great for snacking and dipping, these chips are usually fried, but this is a healthier baked version.

Makes 1 to 2 cups

1 green plantain
1 teaspoon red palm oil or light vegetable oil
1 teaspoon Nététou-Selim Smoked Salt (page 219) or fine sea salt

» Preheat the oven to 350°F.

» With a sharp knife, trim off the ends of the plantain and cut away the skin from the flesh. Slice the plantain on a sharp angle into thin chips with a knife or a mandoline. Toss the plantain slices with the oil and spread in a single layer on a rimmed baking sheet.

» Bake for 20 to 25 minutes, until crisp, flipping once. Toss with the salt while still hot. Serve warm, or store in an airtight container for up to 2 weeks once cooled.

SELIM-CRUSTED SALMON

with PLANTAIN PURÉE & SAUCE MOYO

SAUCE MOYO

- 1 Scotch bonnet pepper, seeded and finely chopped
- 1 tablespoon chopped fresh parsley
- 1 tablespoon finely chopped chives
- Juice of 1 lime
- 2 garlic cloves, finely chopped
- 2 cups seeded, chopped plum tomatoes
- 1 red onion, thinly sliced
- 2 tablespoons vegetable oil
- Salt and freshly ground black pepper

PLANTAIN PURÉE

- 1 green plantain, peeled and coarsely chopped
- 3 ripe plantains, peeled and coarsely chopped
- 2 tablespoons red palm oil or vegetable oil, plus more if needed

SALMON

- 2 tablespoons Touba Spice Mix (recipe follows)
- 4 (8-ounce) skin-on salmon fillets
- 2 tablespoons vegetable oil

I fell in love with the unique kick of *selim* pepper while enjoying café Touba in the bustling streets of Dakar. The rub I created with the pepper works great with salmon and can also be used with chicken. The plantain's mild sweetness goes well with the bright, spicy *moyo* sauce, another quintessential street food condiment. This dish is what happens when comfort food meets street food.

❯❯ **To prepare the sauce:** Combine all the ingredients in a bowl and stir well. Season with salt and pepper. Let sit for an hour for the flavors to develop.

❯❯ **To prepare the plantain purée:** Place the green plantain pieces in one saucepan and the ripe plantain pieces in another. Fill both pots with enough salted water to cover and bring to a boil. Boil both until soft: the ripe plantains will take 5 to 10 minutes; the green plantain will take longer, 15 to 20 minutes.

❯❯ Drain the plantains well and place in a food processor while still hot. Add the oil and process until smooth, adding more oil if needed.

It should have the consistency of mashed potatoes. Season with salt and pepper to taste. Keep warm.

❯❯ **To prepare the salmon:** Generously rub the spice mixture on the flesh side of each fillet, pressing to adhere.

❯❯ In a large nonstick frying pan, heat the oil over medium-high heat. Sear the fillets, skin side down until golden brown and crisp, 3 to 4 minutes. Flip and sear on the flesh side until a crust has formed, another 2 to 3 minutes, or less if you prefer a rarer fillet. Serve hot with the plantain purée and sauce on the side.

TOUBA SPICE MIX

Makes about ¼ cup

- 1 teaspoon ground selim pepper
- 1 tablespoon salt
- 1 teaspoon freshly ground black pepper
- 1 tablespoon cumin (ground or whole)
- 1 teaspoon ground turmeric
- 1 teaspoon cayenne pepper
- Grated zest of 1 lime

❯❯ Combine all the ingredients in a small bowl. Store in an airtight container in a cool, dry place for up to 2 months.

LIME & GREEN TEA–CURED THIOFF

(JOLLOF GRAVLAX)

Aunt Marie, who lived in Sweden when my uncle served as the ambassador of Senegal, inspired this recipe. While there, she fell in love with gravlax, the Scandinavian specialty of cured salmon. Brewed green tea (*attaya*) is Senegal's number one beverage, and is obviously not part of the typical Swedish method for preparing gravlax; however, it adds a certain depth to the cured fish. The green *moringa*-and-mint-infused salt brings an additional depth of flavor and nutrients. The cured fish is great served on toast points or crackers at cocktail parties, or as a first course with a simple green salad.

- 1½ cups sugar
- ½ cup Moringa Mint Salt (page 219) or fine sea salt
- 1 teaspoon freshly ground black pepper
- ½ cup brewed green gunpowder tea, cooled (see Note)
- Grated zest of 2 limes
- 1 cup packed moringa leaves, chopped, or ½ cup moringa powder
- 1 (10- to 12-ounce) skinless thioff fillet or other firm-fleshed fish fillet (such as grouper)

» Combine the sugar, salt, pepper, tea, lime zest, and moringa in a bowl and mix well. Place the fillet on a large deep plate or in a shallow bowl and pack the cure all over. Refrigerate, uncovered, for at least 24 hours. After 24 hours, check if the fish is tender; if not, allow a few hours more to cure.

» Before serving, scrape off the cure, but do not rinse the fillet; some spice mixture should remain. Cut very thin slices of the fish on an angle with a sharp knife. Serve immediately or wrap well in plastic wrap and refrigerate for up to 1 week.

NOTE: *To make the green tea, bring 1 cup water to a boil, let it sit off the heat for a moment, then pour it over 1 heaping teaspoon tea leaves. Let steep for 3 minutes, then strain.*

THIEBOU JENN

- 1 large whole thioff or grouper (about 5 pounds), scaled, gutted, and cut into 7 steaks about 1½ inches thick, reserving the head and tail
- 1 cup Rof (recipe follows)
- ½ cup vegetable oil
- Salt
- 2 white onions, chopped
- 1 green bell pepper, seeded and chopped
- 2 cups tomato paste
- 5 cups water
- 1 cup dried white hibiscus flowers (optional)
- 2 whole Scotch bonnet peppers
- Freshly ground black pepper
- 2 palm-size pieces guedj (see Note)
- 2 pieces yeet, rinsed (see Note)
- ½ head green cabbage, cut into 3 wedges
- 1 turnip, peeled and cut into thick wedges
- 1 globe eggplant, halved lengthwise
- 1 small butternut squash, peeled, seeded, and cut into large chunks
- 1 yuca (4 to 5 inches long), peeled and cut into large chunks
- 2 carrots, peeled and cut into large chunks
- 2 bitter eggplants (optional)
- ¼ pound small whole okra pods, trimmed
- 1 handful shelled tamarind pods or 1 tablespoon tamarind paste
- 2 cups broken white rice, or jasmine or basmati rice, washed and drained
- 2 limes, cut into wedges

This is the one dish that unites all Senegalese. *Thiebou jenn*, our national dish, is served daily in many Senegalese households, each with their own special recipe. Though very traditional, no Senegalese cookbook would be complete without a *thiebou jenn* recipe. This version calls for certain ingredients that may not be accessible in many Western markets, but that shouldn't discourage you, as Vietnamese or Thai fish sauce is a good substitute that will bring the fermented flavor characteristic of *thiebou jenn*.

The selection of root vegetables to be used is up to you. Traditionally *thioff*, a very popular fish in Senegal, is used in *thiebou jenn*, but any firm-fleshed fish such as grouper, sea bass, haddock, or halibut will work. If you have your fishmonger cut your whole fish into steaks, make sure you keep the head and tail to add to the pot. There are many different ways to prepare *thiebou jenn* and this is a slightly more traditional version than the recipe in my first cookbook, *Yolele!*. The *thiebou jenn* in the photo opposite is yet another version I enjoyed at the lively Chez Loutcha in Dakar in which the fish is kept whole and fried.

○

NOTE: *If you can't find* guedj *and* yeet *(see page 70), substitute with Vietnamese or Thai fish sauce, using about a total of ¼ to ½ cup, to taste.*

》 Cut two 2-inch-long slits into the meaty part of each fish steak. Stuff each slit with about 1 teaspoon of the rof. Place the fish, including the head and tail, in a shallow bowl or baking dish and coat with the remaining rof. Cover and refrigerate until needed.

》 Heat the vegetable oil in a large pot over medium-high heat. Add 2 pinches of salt, the onions, green pepper, and tomato paste. Reduce the heat to low and stir well. Stirring occasionally to avoid scorching, cook for 10 to 15 minutes, until the vegetables are soft and the tomato paste turns a dark orange. (You may need to add 1 to 2 tablespoons water to further prevent scorching.)

》 Add the water and stir well. The paste will thin out and become sauce-like. Return to a boil, reduce the heat, and simmer for about 30 minutes, until the oil separates and rises to the surface.

》 Carefully add the fish steaks, including the head and tail, along with the hibiscus (if using), Scotch bonnets, and a pinch of black pepper. Cook uncovered over medium heat for about 15 minutes, until the fish is cooked.

》 Carefully remove the fish and set aside in a large bowl. Cover and keep warm. Add the guedj and yeet (or ¼ to ½ cup fish sauce) to the pot. Partially cover the pot, leaving the lid ajar, and simmer for 10 minutes.

》 Add the cabbage, turnip, eggplant halves, squash, yuca, carrots, and bitter eggplants (if

(recipe continues)

using). Return to a boil and season with salt and pepper. Reduce the heat and simmer for another 20 minutes. Add the okra and cook for 10 more minutes, until the vegetables are tender.

>> Remove the vegetables and place in the bowl of fish. Add a few ladles of broth and the tamarind.

>> Line a large colander with cheesecloth and add the washed rice. Place over the simmering broth and cover. Let steam for 10 to 15 minutes.

>> Add the rice to the broth and give it a big stir. Bring to a boil, then reduce the heat to low. Use a ladle to skim the excess oil from the top; discard the oil. There should be just enough broth to cover the rice; if not, remove the excess broth with the ladle. Tightly cover with a lid and cook until the rice is tender and the liquid absorbed, about 20 minutes.

>> When the rice is finished, arrange the rice on a large platter. Scrape the crust from the bottom of the pot and place in a bowl to be served on the side. Arrange the fish and vegetables in the center of the rice. Serve with lime wedges.

ROF

Makes about 1 cup

3 garlic cloves
1 bunch parsley, coarsely chopped
1 white onion, coarsely chopped
3 scallions, chopped
1 vegetable or fish bouillon cube (optional)
1 tablespoon chile flakes
1 tablespoon freshly ground black pepper

>> Place all the ingredients in a food processor and pulse until coarse, or pound in a mortar with a pestle.

THIEBOU JENN ALSO SPEAKS TO ME

Amadou Elimane Kane is a Senegalese poet laureate, writer, and scholar who lives and teaches in Paris. He is a Pan-African activist who founded the Pan-African Cultural Institute. In this beautiful ode to our national dish *thiebou jenn*, Mr. Kane sings the "sun-color flavors" that dissipate the night forever. Through Mr. Kane's words, *thiebou jenn* becomes a true feast of the senses, symbolizing a promise of freedom and renaissance. I am indebted to Mr. Kane for his generosity, as he wrote this poem especially for this book.

THIEBOU JENN ALSO SPEAKS TO ME

I see light in your creativity
I sing the sun-color flavors
Color of light
Where runoff beauty delights
And you saved us from loneliness
I look at the fruity burst
In your hot breath
Glittering generosity
Between your paths opens the zest
Fecund and primal
A perfume of rebirth
Henceforth night no longer exists

Of your creativity
Hot curves
follow
To spread in the thousands
In the cradle of my land
Africa
From this sky with fertile horizon
And mouths ajar
Singing this song of freedom
The sweet melody that tells me about my dreams
Tells the sheer roundness of your geometry
That traces your fingers of light
Henceforth, night no longer exists

This scent of ripe mango
Where senses enliven
This delicious beauty
Where suns meet
Powerful nature of scents
Bursting on earth
My earth

And the prints of your balsamic fingers
Where rainbow colors flow
On the edge of your nurturing geometries
Shining with peace
Sharing
And freedom

Your garden
Where are picked
Pieces of rainbow
Your garden
Eternal beauty
Purple and juicy light
Your garden
Fragrance of mango
Taste of baobab in bloom
The trees sap of creativity
Open lemony songs
To the Renaissance
To freedom
Henceforth, night no longer exists

In the glare of your gardens
This promise takes us
In a calabash of solidarity
When this time
Where in the suavity of light
Draws the sweet baobab
Cut the ripe fruit
Thy scented fingers
Mouthful plural and hot
Henceforth, night no longer exists

TRANSLATED FROM THE FRENCH BY PIERRE THIAM

LE THIEBOU DIÈNE AUSSI ME PARLE

Je vois lumière à ta créativité
Je chante les saveurs couleur de soleil
Couleur lumière
Où ruisselle la beauté des délices
Et tu nous délivres de la solitude
Je regarde l'élan fruité
À ton souffle épicé
Scintillant de générosité
Entre tes allées s'ouvre l'éclat
Fécond et originel
Un parfum de renaissance
La nuit désormais n'existe plus

De ta créativité
Des courbes chaudes
Se suivent
Pour se répandre en milliers
Dans le berceau de ma terre
La terre africaine
De ce ciel à l'horizon fertile
Aux bouches entrouvertes
Qui entonnent ce chant de liberté
La mélopée sucrée qui me parle de mes rêves
Raconte la rondeur diaphane de ta géométrie
Que tracent tes doigts de lumière
La nuit désormais n'existe plus

Ce parfum de mangue mûre
Où vont s'égayer les sens
Cette beauté savoureuse
Où se rencontrent les soleils
Nature puissante des effluves
Qui éclatent sur la terre
Ma terre

Et de l'empreinte de tes doigts balsamiques
Où coulent les couleurs arc-en-ciel
À la lisière de tes géométries nourricières
Luisantes de paix
                    De partage
                              Et de liberté

Ton jardin
Où se cueillent
Des morceaux d'arc-en-ciel
Ton jardin
Beauté d'éternité
Lumière pourpre et juteuse
Ton jardin
Parfum de mangue
Goût de baobab fleuri
Les arbres sève de créativité
Ouvrent les chants citronnés
Vers la Renaissance
Vers la liberté
La nuit désormais n'existe plus

Dans l'éblouissement de tes jardins
Cette promesse nous transporte
Dans une calebasse de solidarité
Quand cet instant
Où dans la suavité de la lumière
Dessine le baobab sucré
Découpe le fruit mûr
De tes doigts parfumés
Bouchée plurielle et chaude
La nuit désormais n'existe plus

AMADOU ELIMANE KANE

GRILLED OYSTERS CASAMANCE

12 Blue Point oysters
Lime wedges
Tomato Onion Relish (recipe follows), for serving
Steamed white rice, for serving (optional)

From about February to the end of June in Casamance, oysters abound, clinging to the roots of mangrove trees. They are most often enjoyed simply boiled or grilled over wood fires right on the river bank after harvesting. I cannot say which method I prefer as they are both delicious. Since my first cookbook, *Yolele!*, included my relative's boiled oyster recipe, Oysters Elinkine, here's the super simple recipe for grilled oysters, which we like to eat with white rice to catch all the light, smoky oyster juices.

» Preheat the grill to hot. If your oysters are on the small side, punch a large piece of aluminum foil with a few holes and place over the grill grates to prevent the oysters from slipping through.

» Place the closed oysters cup side down (the curved side) on the grill. Be cautious, as occasionally oysters can explode or shatter if the grill is too hot. Close the grill cover or tent the oysters with another piece of foil. Grill for about 5 minutes, a little longer for larger oysters, until the oysters are just cooked through and their shells loosen and open. Be careful not to overcook them. Also note that the shells will open only slightly (not as wide as clams and mussels), and once taken off the grill, you will have to remove the top shell.

» Using a sharp knife, cut the oyster from the bottom shell. Serve hot or warm with lime wedges, relish, and rice (if you like), topped with the lightly smoked oyster juices that collect in the grilled shells.

TOMATO ONION RELISH

Makes about 2 cups

½ **red onion, thinly sliced**
Juice of 2 limes
1 yellow tomato, diced
1 red tomato, diced
1 Scotch bonnet pepper, seeded and finely chopped
½ **cup vegetable oil**
Fine sea salt and freshly ground pepper
¼ **cup chopped fresh cilantro**

» In a bowl, combine the onion, lime juice, tomatoes, Scotch bonnet, and oil. Stir to mix well. Season with salt and pepper to taste. Just before serving, fold in the cilantro.

COCONUT MUSSELS

with CRISPY YUCA FRIES

- 2 tablespoons red palm oil or vegetable oil
- 3 shallots, thinly sliced
- 1 tablespoon peeled, minced fresh ginger
- 2 garlic cloves, minced
- 2 tablespoons ground cumin
- 1 teaspoon ground turmeric
- 1 tablespoon cayenne pepper
- 1 tablespoon tomato paste
- 1 tablespoon light brown sugar
- 2 cups full-fat coconut milk
- 2 tablespoons Vietnamese or Thai fish sauce
- 4 pounds fresh mussels, purged and scrubbed
- 1 tablespoon tamarind paste
- 2 tablespoons chopped fresh cilantro
- Juice of 1 lime
- Crispy Yuca Fries (recipe follows)

This is a Senegalese nod to the Belgian classic, *moules frites*. The mussels must be live; discard any that don't remain closed after you press the shells with your fingers—those are dead. This recipe is a crowd pleaser, so be sure to have enough yuca fries to soak up the broth once all the mussels are eaten.

❯❯ In a large pan with a tightly fitting lid, heat the oil over medium heat. Gently cook the shallots, ginger, garlic, cumin, turmeric, cayenne, and tomato paste until fragrant, 3 to 5 minutes. Stir frequently to avoid scorching.

❯❯ Add the sugar and stir well. Add the coconut milk and bring to a boil, stirring often. Add the fish sauce. Taste and adjust the seasoning with more fish sauce if needed.

❯❯ Gently add the mussels to the sauce and tightly cover with a lid. Cook for 3 to 4 minutes, until the mussels open. Discard any that remain closed. Be careful not to overcook them, or the mussels will shrink and become rubbery. Turn off the heat and stir in the tamarind, cilantro, and lime juice.

❯❯ Transfer the mussels and sauce to a large serving bowl and serve hot with yuca fries on the side.

CRISPY YUCA FRIES

Yuca fries are easy to prepare, and I find them so much tastier than french fries. I like to serve them cut into thick pieces, which renders them crisp on the outside and soft and moist inside. The length of cooking time for yuca depends on its age and quality; the ones in Senegal tend to take much longer than the yuca bought in the U.S.

Serves 4

2 pounds yuca, peeled and cut into 3- to 4-inch-long pieces
Vegetable oil, for frying
2 tablespoons Nététou-Selim Smoked Salt (page 219) or fine sea salt

❯❯ Place the yuca in a large pot and cover with salted water. Bring to a boil, reduce the heat to medium, and cook until the yuca is tender but not falling apart, 10 to 15 minutes. Drain well and let cool until it is easy to handle. Remove and discard the string-like fibrous core. Cut the yuca into thick batons, ½- to ¾-inch thick. Set aside on paper towels to dry.

❯❯ Line a large bowl with paper towels. Pour oil into a large, deep cast-iron skillet or other heavy pot to a depth of 2 inches, and heat to 375°F over medium-high heat.

❯❯ Carefully drop the yuca into the oil without overcrowding. Using a slotted spoon, separate the fries in the oil. Fry until crisp and golden, turning once, 2 to 3 minutes total. Remove and drain in the paper towel–lined bowl. Repeat with the remaining yuca. Season the fries with the salt and serve hot.

MUSSELS MAFÉ

SERVES
2

AUTHOR'S NOTE:

*Eric Simeon is a New York–
based chef who joined me on
the Senegalese culinary tour,
AfroEats. I first met Eric during
a trip to the stunning Victoria
Falls in Zimbabwe where we were
both panelists at a conference
on the topic of culinary tourism.
Eric had previously traveled
throughout West Africa and
fallen in love with the food.
Needless to say, we became
instant friends.*

2 tablespoons peanut oil

1 leek, sliced into ⅛-inch
   rounds

1 3-inch piece fresh ginger,
   peeled and grated

2 garlic cloves, minced

2 tablespoons tomato paste

1 cup water

1 tablespoon shrimp paste
   (see Note)

½ cup unsweetened smooth
   peanut butter

1 quart chicken stock

1 small kohlrabi, peeled and
   cut into 12 wedges

1 pound kabocha squash,
   peeled, seeded, and cut
   into large dice

½ head savoy cabbage, cut
   into 1½-inch squares

4 Thai bird chiles, minced

10 whole okra pods

Salt and freshly ground black
   pepper

1 pound mussels, purged and
   scrubbed

1 bunch fresh cilantro, leaves
   chopped

Juice of 1 lime

Salt and freshly ground black
   pepper

Crusty baguette, for serving

I t was my junior year of college in Accra, Ghana, and I was totally addicted to the food: *fufu*, *banku*, *kenkey*, palm nut, and the ceremony of eating with your hand out of a large wooden bowl, sitting outside on a plain wooden bench with dirt under your feet and huge cauldrons of soup boiling away next to you. To this day, spicy peanut soup with *fufu* is my greatest comfort food.

I traveled to Senegal that same year, and was destined to love *mafé*, but it wasn't until my last visit to Dakar that I was introduced to the amazing wealth of seafood that Senegal has to offer. To this I added my experiences in Maine (local mussels) and Hawaii (Asian ingredients), and created this dish, thinking that it would be perfect to eat on the Pointe des Almadies. —*Eric Simeon*

◉

❯❯ Heat the oil in a large saucepan over medium heat. Add the leek, ginger, and garlic and cook, stirring frequently, until the leek is soft, about 3 minutes.

❯❯ Stir in the tomato paste and water, and cook for 3 minutes more. Add the shrimp paste and peanut butter and stir until completely incorporated.

❯❯ Stir in the chicken stock and bring to a simmer. Add the kohlrabi, squash, cabbage, and chiles, cover, and simmer until the squash is soft, about 10 minutes.

❯❯ While the vegetables are cooking, prepare the okra. Trim the stems and season with salt and pepper. Heat a large cast-iron skillet on high heat. Add the okra in a single layer and sear for 2 minutes. Turn each pod and continue cooking to char the other side.

❯❯ When the squash is soft, add the mussels and re-cover the pan. Let them simmer for about 2 minutes. Stir the mussels and continue steaming until all of them open. Discard any that remain closed.

❯❯ Stir in the okra, cilantro, and lime juice. Adjust the seasoning with salt and pepper to taste. Serve with a crusty baguette.

NOTE: *For this recipe I used Malaysian shrimp paste, but only because I had no* nététou *or* yeet. *If you can find either, use the same amount instead.*

FONIO-CRUSTED CRAB CAKES

Crabs from the Senegal River are similar to the Dungeness variety, large and plump with sweet and tender flesh. In the northern city of Saint-Louis, they are usually cooked whole in a spicy tomato broth (*coti*). That dish is full of flavor and fun to eat with your hands, but there is so much work involved in getting the meat out of the crab shells.

An easier way to enjoy crab is by making these wonderful crab cakes. You can either steam crabs and pull the meat out of the shells ahead of time, or simply buy fresh crabmeat from your supermarket or fishmonger.

◉

» Place the plantain pieces in a pot and cover with salted water. Bring to a boil and cook until the plantain is very soft and easily pierced with a fork, 15 to 20 minutes. Drain well. Place in a large bowl, add the palm oil, and mash with a fork until smooth. Set aside to cool.

» Add the egg, 1 tablespoon fonio, the onion, cilantro, lime juice, salt, and pepper to the mashed plantain and mix well. Gently fold in the crab. Using your hands, shape into 12 cakes.

» On a wide plate, combine the flour and ⅔ cup fonio. Dredge the crab cakes in the fonio-flour mixture and set on a baking sheet or platter. Cover with plastic wrap and refrigerate for 1 to 3 hours to set.

» Line a platter with several layers of paper towels. Pour vegetable oil into a large frying pan to a depth of ¼ inch, and heat to 375°F over medium-high heat. Gently fry a few crab cakes at a time until golden brown, 2 to 3 minutes each side. Set aside on the paper towels to drain. Repeat until all the cakes are fried.

» Serve hot with lime wedges and mango salsa or ginger dressing on the side.

1 large green plantain, peeled and cut into small chunks

1 tablespoon red palm oil or vegetable oil

1 large egg, beaten

⅔ cup plus 1 tablespoon cooked fonio (page 150) or quinoa

1 tablespoon finely chopped yellow onion

1 tablespoon finely chopped fresh cilantro

½ teaspoon lime juice

⅛ teaspoon fine sea salt

⅛ teaspoon freshly ground black pepper

1 pound fresh lump crabmeat, picked over

¼ cup all-purpose flour

Vegetable oil, for frying

Lime wedges, for serving

Mango Salsa (page 196) or Ginger Dressing (page 129), for serving

THE THREAT OF FISH FACTORIES

I remember Joal!
I remember signares in the green darkness of verandas,
Signares with eyes surreal as shafts of moonlight on the sand.

—An excerpt from "Joal" by our late poet-president, **LÉOPOLD SÉDAR SENGHOR**.

Once a small fishing village, Joal is famously known as the birthplace of Senegal's first president, L. S. Senghor, who immortalized it in his poem "Joal." It is now a city of 40,000 inhabitants and the largest traditional fishing port in the country. Working with the Senegalese fishermen who come to Joal to unload their catch, women dominate the traditional process of drying, curing, and smoking fish to be used in many traditional dishes (see page 70). Sadly, the artisans have been hampered by the foreign fish-processing factories sprouting up all along the coast near the fishing ports.

When the foreign factories first arrived, they mostly bought up catches of conch and other small fish that did not feature prominently in the Senegalese diet. Now, they've begun to buy up *yaboy* (sardines, called *kobo* in Casamance) and other small fish that locals consume. The foreign factories process the fish into meal to be used at fish farms abroad, and local fish prices have skyrocketed. In these already-depleted waters, there is simply not enough fish to go around, and the Senegalese artisans are being pushed out of Joal. It will mean the death of small traditional industries that produce the funky fish products key to our local cuisine.

What will happen when our fishermen no longer have any reason to go fishing? When communities that have lived for centuries on artisanal fishing are no longer able to meet their needs? Many have already left fishing behind to participate in the lucrative trafficking of illegal immigrants, using their rickety fishing boats to smuggle thousands willing to risk their lives in search of jobs in Europe.

GRILLED PIRI PIRI PRAWNS
& WATERMELON SALAD

SERVES
6
AS A STARTER

PRAWNS

¼ cup vegetable oil

4 garlic cloves, finely chopped

1 Scotch bonnet pepper, finely
chopped, or 2 tablespoons
cayenne pepper

1 teaspoon fine sea salt

1 teaspoon sweet paprika

18 prawns (shells and heads
on, if possible) or large
shrimp

WATERMELON SALAD

6 large wedges watermelon,
about 1½ inches thick
(rind on)

½ cup olive oil, plus more for
brushing

Juice of 2 limes

1 tablespoon fine sea salt

1 teaspoon freshly ground
black pepper

½ cup thinly sliced red onion

1 large jicama, peeled and cut
into ½-inch cubes
(see Note)

2 tablespoons chopped fresh
cilantro

2 tablespoons chopped fresh
mint

Pinch of Hibiscus-Chile Salt
(page 219; optional)

NOTE: *Jicama can be found
in Latin American markets, but
cucumber may be used instead.*

This fiery piri piri recipe is Mozambican-inspired and it is, to me, the best way to serve prawns. If you prefer, the heat of the marinade can be toned down by using less Scotch bonnet, but don't fear, the watermelon's fresh sweetness will attenuate its burning effect. I like to serve the prawns with the shells on to keep all the flavors, so I encourage eating with your fingers, which I'm sure you'll be licking clean.

》 To prepare the prawns:
Combine the vegetable oil, garlic, Scotch bonnet, salt, and paprika in a large bowl. Add the prawns and toss well. Cover and marinate in the refrigerator for at least 2 hours or up to 24 hours.

》 To prepare the salad: Preheat the grill or a grill pan to hot.

》 Blot the watermelon wedges with paper towels to remove excess juice. Lightly brush with olive oil and grill for 1 to 2 minutes on each side, until lightly charred. Set aside to cool. Cut off and discard the watermelon rind. Cut the flesh into 1-inch chunks.

》 In a large bowl, combine the lime juice, salt, and pepper. Slowly add the olive oil, whisking constantly to emulsify. Taste and adjust the seasoning. Add the onion, watermelon, jicama, and 1 tablespoon each cilantro and mint. Toss well.

》 Drain the prawns and discard any leftover marinade. Grill the prawns for 2 to 3 minutes on each side until just pink.

》 To serve, spoon a serving of salad into each bowl and arrange the grilled prawns on top. Top with the remaining mint and cilantro and a pinch of hibiscus salt. Serve immediately.

SENEGALESE
FLAVORED SALTS

I love to infuse salt with natural Senegalese ingredients, particularly the salt from the Pink Lake. It's a very easy way to bring new flavors to a dish when used as a finishing salt added right before serving. Try them on soups, grilled meats, eggs, toasts, even desserts and cocktails. These salts have the added benefit of being beautifully colored, too.

The process for creating flavored salts couldn't be easier. First, make sure all your ingredients are dry and ground, chopped, or flaked. You can dry herbs or citrus zest in a low oven (150° to 200°F) or in a dehydrator.

For each salt, combine all the ingredients in a small bowl. Each recipe makes about ¼ cup salt, which can be stored in an airtight container for up to a year.

NOTE: *Smoking your own sea salt is quite easy. Soak a cup of wood chips in water for 1 hour. For easier cleanup, line a roasting pan with heavy-duty aluminum foil. Drain the wood chips, scatter them in the roasting pan, and place the roasting rack on top. Spread the salt on a sheet of aluminum foil on top of the rack. Loosely cover the pan and place it on the stove over medium-high heat. When the chips start smoking, tightly cover the pan, reduce the heat to medium, and smoke for about 1 hour, until well-infused. Allow the salt to cool. Store in an airtight container.*

HIBISCUS-CHILE SALT

This lovely purple-colored salt is spicy and acidic. It looks and tastes amazing on soups or on a fruit salad.

¼ cup fine or flaked sea salt
1 teaspoon coarsely ground dried red hibiscus flowers
½ teaspoon sweet paprika
½ teaspoon chile flakes or ground chile

MORINGA MINT SALT

This salt smells incredible from the mint and lime zest, and has a lovely green hue from the *moringa* powder and baobab leaves, both full of nutrients. It looks and tastes lovely, especially on the Coconut-Lime-Palm Ice Cream (page 293).

¼ cup fine or flaked sea salt
½ teaspoon moringa powder
¼ teaspoon ground baobab leaves
½ teaspoon crushed dried mint
1 teaspoon dried grated lime zest

NÉTÉTOU-SELIM SMOKED SALT

Smoky and pungent—I love the intensity of this salt. Try it on grilled meats, oily fish, or rich stews.

¼ cup smoked fine or flaked sea salt (see Note)
¼ teaspoon nététou powder
¼ teaspoon ground selim pepper
1 teaspoon freshly ground black pepper

THE PINK LAKE

About an hour's drive northeast of Dakar, amidst the dusty roads, lies an unlikely natural wonder: a shimmering pink lake. One of the only living creatures in Lac Rose, officially named Lake Retba, is an algae that produces a magenta pigment, making the lake appear pink, especially in the dry season. The very high salt content allows people to effortlessly float in the water, as at the Dead Sea. It's a popular tourist destination, but for many locals and West Africans from all over the region, harvesting salt from the lake is a way of life. The salt, extracted by hand in back-breaking work, is mostly destined for the local market or exported to other West African countries.

At certain times of the year, I come foraging for sea beans, also known as salicornia or samphire. The bushes of sea beans, with their unique pinkish hue, are the only plantlife that thrives wild here, growing abundantly on the lake's shore. I enjoy picking the tender tips under the amused look of the locals, who don't eat them. I love their crunchy, salty, briny flavor in a simply dressed salad.

On our AfroEats trip (see page 53), we boarded several boats and rowed to the middle of the lake. The boats have flat wooden bottoms, specially designed to carry heavy loads of extracted salt. From there, we watched Camara, a Guinea native, dive into the water, carrying a large woven basket. He came back up with a full basket heavy with greyish salt, which he emptied onto the floor of an empty boat. He dove again, repeating the process until the boat was full of salt crystals. Camara is in the water for about eight hours a day and uses shea butter to protect his skin from the harsh salt water.

Once the boat was full, he returned to the shore where his partners, often family members, helped him haul the salt to large piles along the bank. A daily salt harvest can be up to one ton. I have become addicted to the Pink Lake's salt and have developed a number of flavored salt recipes to complement it (page 219).

MEAT

SLOW-ROASTED
LEG OF LAMB, DIBI-STYLE

1 bone-in leg of lamb (6 to 7½ pounds)

3 sprigs thyme, leaves chopped

10 garlic cloves, cut into thick slivers

2 tablespoons Dijon mustard, plus more for serving

2 tablespoons ground cumin

2 tablespoons salt

2 tablespoons freshly ground black pepper

2 tablespoons vegetable oil

2 large yellow onions, thinly sliced

¼ cup water

Baguettes, for serving

Tamarind Kani Sauce (recipe follows), for serving

NOTE: *Instead of a sheet of kraft paper, you can also place the lamb inside a large, clean paper grocery bag and tie the opening closed with kitchen twine. Other options include using a double layer of parchment paper or aluminum foil, or even an ovenproof casserole with a tightly fitting lid. Be sure **not** to use wax paper.*

In *dibiteries* in Senegal, meat is wrapped in kraft paper and placed in the back of wood-burning clay ovens or on coals in a hole, covered, and slowly cooked until tender and succulent. At home, you can replicate the process in a low oven. The leg will cook for the better part of the day, but your patience will pay off in slabs of juicy meat, falling off the bone. It's very easy to put together as all the work is done in the oven; though it takes 8 hours to roast, it will probably take you only about 15 minutes to prepare it. Toward the end of the cooking time, your house will smell heavenly. The meat is so tender it can be eaten with spoons. Make sure to have some baguettes to mop up the juices and extra Dijon mustard and Tamarind Kani Sauce on the side.

》 Preheat the oven to 175°F.

》 Trim some of the excess fat from the lamb, but not all of it. With a paring knife, cut deep slits into the lamb. Generously stuff chopped thyme and garlic in the slits. In a bowl, combine the mustard, cumin, salt, pepper, and oil. Rub the mixture all over the leg of lamb.

》 Line a baking sheet with a piece of kraft paper large enough to enclose the lamb and onions. Spread the onions in a layer in the center of the paper and lay the lamb on top. Carefully pour the water around the leg. Fold the paper tightly around the lamb and onions, enclosing them like a package. Make sure that the paper is completely sealed closed. Place the lamb, on the baking sheet, in the oven and roast for 8 hours. The lamb is done when the meat pulls away and is spoon-tender.

》 Serve from the paper or on a platter with baguette chunks to mop up the juices and extra mustard and the kani sauce on the side.

TAMARIND KANI SAUCE

Every Senegalese household has a *kani* sauce and this one's mine. You'll find this fiery sauce on just about every table in Senegal, especially at *dibiteries*. Though you can buy it bottled, I feel it's worthwhile making your own. As a kid I used to love the street snack *paañ niambaan*, spicy dried clams flavored with tamarind. I've taken those tangy, sweet, deep flavors to my version of *kani*. It's a great spicy condiment that can be served with pretty much anything—just like ketchup!

Makes about 1 cup

1 tablespoon peanut oil
1 yellow onion, coarsely chopped
1 garlic clove, chopped
6 plum tomatoes, coarsely chopped
1 Scotch bonnet pepper, coarsely chopped
1 dried bay leaf
2 tablespoons tamarind paste
1 tablespoon sugar
2 tablespoons Vietnamese or Thai fish sauce
Salt and freshly ground black pepper

» In a saucepan, heat the oil over medium-low heat. Cook the onion and garlic, stirring frequently, until soft and fragrant. Add the tomatoes, Scotch bonnet, and bay leaf. Simmer for 15 minutes, or until thick like a chutney, stirring occasionally with a wooden spoon and adding a little water if necessary.

» Add the tamarind, sugar, and fish sauce and season with salt and pepper to taste. Remove the bay leaf and purée in a food processor or blender until smooth. Store in the refrigerator in an airtight container for up to 3 weeks.

YASSA LAMB BURGER

BURGERS

2 pounds ground lamb (not too lean)

2 garlic cloves, minced

1 yellow onion, finely chopped

Grated zest of 1 lime

1 teaspoon cayenne pepper

2 tablespoons chopped fresh thyme leaves

1 tablespoon salt

2 teaspoons freshly ground black pepper

Vegetable oil, for brushing

YASSA ONIONS

1 tablespoon vegetable oil

2 cups thinly sliced yellow onions

1 dried bay leaf

1 teaspoon salt

1 teaspoon freshly ground black pepper

Juice of 1 lime

6 to 8 buns or several baguettes

OPTIONAL TOPPINGS

Fried eggs

Dijon mustard

Tamarind Kani Sauce (page 229)

Senegalese love lamb. Among our most popular snack destinations are the *dibiteries* (see page 234), casual joints that sell simply grilled lamb. Topped with the onions of *yassa*, another famed Senegalese dish, this delicious lamb burger is a marriage of Senegal's best.

Made with caramelized onions and lime juice, the *yassa* sauce has a sweet and acidic taste, so there is no need for pickles. Many Senegalese argue that there should be mustard in the *yassa* sauce, but in Casamance, where the dish originates, people would disagree quite passionately. However, a good, spicy Dijon mustard with this lamb burger is a great idea. If you like it even spicier, you can opt for the Tamarind Kani Sauce on page 229. In popular shawarma joints of Dakar, burgers are always served topped with a fried egg, which is also an excellent way to serve this one.

》 To prepare the burgers: Place the lamb in a large bowl and add the garlic, onion, lime zest, cayenne, thyme, salt, and black pepper. Using your hands, mix until well-combined. Shape into 6 to 8 burgers. Place on a platter, cover with plastic wrap, and refrigerate for 1 hour.

》 To prepare the onions: Heat the oil in a cast-iron skillet over medium heat. Add the onions and bay leaf and stir well to coat. Season with salt and pepper. Cover and cook undisturbed for 10 to 15 minutes, until soft. Add the lime juice and stir well. Adjust the seasoning and raise the heat to medium-high. Cook the onions uncovered for another 10 minutes or more, stirring from time to time to avoid scorching, until the onions are a nice golden brown. Remove the bay leaf and adjust the seasoning.

》 Preheat the grill or a grill pan to hot.

》 Brush the burgers with a little oil to avoid sticking. Cook the burgers to your desired temperature. Set aside to rest for a few minutes before serving.

》 To serve, top with the yassa onions in a bun or sandwiched in a baguette. Top each with a fried egg and a little mustard or kani sauce, if you'd like.

GOAT CHEESE–STUFFED LAMB MEATBALLS

with MINT-YOGURT SAUCE

Senegal and Morocco have a long history of trading recipes. Rumor has it that Morocco's national dish of couscous was inspired by our own millet couscous (I heard it from the great Paula Wolfert herself, who is considered *the* authority on the food of Morocco).

Thus armed with this knowledge, I give you Moroccan *kefta*–inspired lamb meatballs. Spicy and filling, I stuffed mine with goat cheese sourced from Keur Moussa Monastery (see page 268). They are the perfect snack for grilling, and are great for parties. The mint-yogurt sauce for dipping was inspired by the Lebanese community that's been living in Senegal for several generations now.

》 To prepare the meatballs: Combine the lamb, parsley, cilantro, mint, onion, cumin, cayenne, paprika, black pepper, eggs, and salt in a large bowl and mix well. Tightly cover with plastic wrap and refrigerate for at least an hour.

》 Using your hands, make a round meatball the size of a golf ball, then slightly flatten it into a disk. Put a pinch of goat cheese in the center and carefully wrap the meat around it, gently reshaping it into a ball. Repeat until all the meatballs are filled with goat cheese. Refrigerate again for an hour to firm up until you're ready to cook.

》 To prepare the sauce: Combine the yogurt, mint, garlic, lemon juice, and oil in a bowl. Season with salt and pepper to taste.

》 Preheat the grill or broiler to hot.

》 Grill the meatballs or place them on a baking sheet to broil. You may also pan-fry them in a few tablespoons of oil. Cook, turning a few times, until all sides are browned, 7 to 8 minutes. Serve immediately with the yogurt sauce for dipping.

MEATBALLS

- 2 pounds ground lamb
- ¼ cup chopped fresh parsley
- ¼ cup chopped fresh cilantro
- ¼ cup chopped fresh mint
- 1 yellow onion, finely chopped
- 2 teaspoons ground cumin
- 2 teaspoons cayenne pepper
- 2 teaspoons smoked Spanish paprika
- 2 teaspoons freshly ground black pepper
- 2 large eggs, lightly beaten
- 2 tablespoons fine sea salt
- 1 cup fresh goat cheese

MINT-YOGURT SAUCE

- 1 cup plain full-fat Greek-style yogurt
- 1 cup chopped fresh mint
- 1 garlic clove, minced
- 1 teaspoon lemon juice
- 1 tablespoon olive oil
- Fine sea salt and freshly ground black pepper

LAMB FOR BREAKFAST AT "NO NAME" DIBITERIE

Hidden away in unmarked holes-in-the-wall or shacks are *dibiteries* serving some of the best street food that Senegal has to offer. *Dibiteries*, which can be found all over Senegal, serve *dibi*, meat or fish cooked by wood fire either in clay ovens or on a grill. Many *dibiteries* have cult-like followings, and my childhood friend Yacine told us about a *dibiterie* that she claimed serves the best roasted lamb in town. She warned us that it's very popular and we would need to get there early because by two in the afternoon, everything will have sold out. Not wanting to miss out, lamb for breakfast sounded just right.

The unmarked *dibiterie* was an unassuming shack, edged by a sandy sidewalk across from a gas station. We entered the partially enclosed space that had no signage. Inside, there were no fussy decorations, only simple long communal wooden benches and tables lined along walls darkened by years of wood-burning smoke. The only other decorations were calendars of years past, displaying portraits of various Sufi Brotherhood spiritual leaders in Senegal.

This nameless place was also menu-less. Lamb is the only thing they serve and the setup couldn't be simpler: tell the cook (who is also the owner) how many kilograms of meat you want, then sit and wait. Big slabs of lamb, including haunches, whole racks of ribs, and bellies tied together with *lakhass* (intestine) were impaled on sharpened wooden branches. These giant kebabs were firmly planted in the sand in the open wood-burning oven built into the corner of the room. Smoke filled the oven and the fire slowly roasted the lamb. While the meat cooked, someone served *attaya*, the traditional green tea that is served everywhere and at any time in Senegal.

When the lamb was ready, it was served in big pieces right off the wooden branch, directly on kraft paper. Alongside it came a dish of tangy pickled onions, Dijon mustard, and smoky-spicy *kani* sauce. Whether you eat *dibi* at home, in a *tangana*, or at a *dibiterie*, there is always *kani*—we like a little heat with our food, and every household has its own *kani* recipe. So tender that it melted in my mouth, this *dibi*, like most others, was best eaten with my hands.

ROASTED RACK OF LAMB

with CRISPY BLACK-EYED PEA & YUCA CAKES

- 2 frenched racks of lamb (1½ pounds each), trimmed of most of their fat
- Fine sea salt and freshly ground black pepper
- 2 garlic cloves, finely chopped
- 2 tablespoons Dijon mustard
- 2 teaspoons finely chopped fresh rosemary
- 1 tablespoon finely chopped fresh thyme
- 2 tablespoons chopped fresh parsley
- 2 tablespoons olive oil
- Ndambe Cakes (recipe follows), for serving
- Sauce Moyo (page 202), for serving

Rack of lamb is probably the easiest part of the lamb to cook. The challenge is to not overcook it—even if you are like most Senegalese and like your meat well done—or you may lose how tender and juicy lamb can be. These chops are marinated with Dijon mustard, rosemary, and thyme, classic herbs for lamb. They're served with crisp cakes of yuca, black-eyed peas, and tomato, and a *moyo* sauce that hails from the Benin-Togo region and is not unlike tomato salsas with which you're probably familiar.

» Preheat the oven to 400°F with a rack in the center position. Season the lamb racks with salt and pepper.

» In a small bowl, combine the garlic, mustard, rosemary, thyme, parsley, and olive oil. Coat the meat with the herb mixture, pressing well.

» Transfer the racks to a roasting pan, curved side up, and roast for about 15 minutes. Loosely cover the racks with aluminum foil and roast for another 5 minutes for medium rare, or 10 minutes for medium, depending on the level of doneness you prefer and thickness of the chops.

» Let the racks rest on a cutting board for about 5 minutes. Cut each rack into double chops or individual chops. Serve with the ndambe cakes and moyo sauce.

NDAMBE CAKES
(CRISPY BLACK-EYED PEA & YUCA CAKES)

Interesting cuisine comes out of poverty. *Ndambe*, considered the poor man's food in Senegal, is deliciously concocted with black-eyed peas and either yuca or sweet potatoes in a tomato broth and served with a baguette. Here, I kept the same ingredients as the traditional recipe, but reduced the stew to a much thicker mixture to fry into crisp, golden brown cakes. They go very well with *moyo* (page 202) or cassava pesto (page 141) on the side.

Makes 6 cakes

1 pound yuca, peeled and cut into big chunks
2 tablespoons vegetable oil
1 yellow onion, finely chopped
2 garlic cloves, minced
1 tablespoon tomato paste
½ cup vegetable stock
1 cup cooked black-eyed peas
2 tablespoons chopped fresh parsley
Salt and freshly ground black pepper
¼ cup red palm oil or vegetable oil

)) Place the yuca in a pot and cover with salted water. Bring to a boil, reduce the heat to medium, and cook until the yuca is tender, 15 to 20 minutes. Drain well and let cool until it is easy to handle. Remove and discard the string-like fibrous core. Cut the yuca into 1-inch cubes.

)) While the yuca is cooking, heat the vegetable oil in a frying pan over medium heat. Add the onion and garlic and cook, stirring, until soft. Add the tomato paste and stock and cook until the liquid is reduced by almost half.

)) Add the cooked yuca, black-eyed peas, and parsley and season with 2 teaspoons salt and 1 teaspoon pepper. Combine well and continue cooking, stirring from time to time, until it forms a chunky mass. Adjust the seasoning and let cool until it is easy to handle.

)) Shape by hand into 6 thick cakes about 3 inches wide, or use ring molds. Place the cakes on a plate, cover loosely with plastic wrap, and chill in the refrigerator for about 1 hour, until they firm up.

)) Preheat the oven to 350°F.

)) In a nonstick frying pan, heat the palm oil over medium heat. Working in batches if necessary, fry the cakes until golden brown and crisp, a few minutes on each side. Place the cakes on a baking sheet and finish cooking in the oven until the center is hot, about 10 minutes. Serve hot.

LAMB SHANK MAFÉ
with ROF GREMOLATA

- 2 tablespoons peanut or vegetable oil, plus more if needed
- 6 lamb shanks (about 1¼ pounds each)
- Salt and freshly ground black pepper
- 2 cups chopped yellow onion
- 2 garlic cloves, minced
- 2 tablespoons tomato paste, mixed with a few tablespoons water
- 2 quarts chicken stock or water
- 2 dried bay leaves
- 1 tablespoon finely chopped fresh thyme
- 1 cup unsweetened smooth peanut butter
- 1 Scotch bonnet pepper
- 2 tablespoons Vietnamese or Thai fish sauce
- Rof Gremolata (recipe follows), for serving
- Spring Vegetable Fonio Pilaf (page 162), for serving

Lamb shanks slowly simmered in peanut sauce are to me the image of comfort food in Senegal, especially when served with steamed rice, couscous, or fonio. I must thank Jenn Sit for the idea of topping the shank with a gremolata just as the Milanese people would do. This gremolata recipe is a twist on our traditional *rof*, the parsley mixture we use to stuff the fish in *thiebou jenn* (page 204). The heat from the Scotch bonnet and brightness of the lemon zest brilliantly lifts all the earthy flavors of the peanut sauce.

» Heat the oil in a large saucepan or Dutch oven over medium-high heat. Season the lamb shanks with salt and pepper. Add the shanks a few at a time, without overcrowding. Brown them well on all sides, about 8 minutes, and set aside on a plate. Repeat until all the shanks are nicely browned, adding more oil if necessary.

» In the same pan, brown the onions. Reduce the heat to low and add the minced garlic. Stir well, then add the diluted tomato paste. Cook, stirring with a wooden spoon, for 7 to 10 minutes, until a deep, dark red. Add another tablespoon or two of water to prevent scorching, if needed.

» Add the stock, raise the heat, and bring to a boil, then reduce to a simmer. Add the bay leaves, thyme, 2 teaspoons salt, and 1 teaspoon

pepper. Slowly add the peanut butter 1 to 2 tablespoons at a time, stirring constantly to dissolve it in the liquid.

» Return the shanks to the pot, pressing down to submerge them in the sauce. Add the Scotch bonnet and fish sauce. Bring to a boil, then reduce the heat to a simmer. Cover and cook for about 1 hour and 30 minutes, until the shanks are tender.

» Uncover the pot and continue cooking until the sauce is thick and coats the back of a spoon. Remove the bay leaves and skim off the fat. Adjust the seasoning.

» Serve the lamb shanks and sauce hot, on a platter. Top each shank with a generous pinch of gremolata and serve with a side of fonio pilaf.

ROF GREMOLATA

Italian gremolata, a condiment traditionally made with herbs, lemon zest, and garlic, meets Senegalese *rof* in this fresh, flavor-packed topping.

Makes about 1 cup

1 bunch parsley, leaves finely chopped
3 scallions, finely chopped
2 garlic cloves, minced
½ Scotch bonnet pepper, seeded and finely chopped
Grated zest of 1 lemon
Fine sea salt and freshly ground black pepper

❱❱ Gently combine the parsley, scallions, garlic, Scotch bonnet, and lemon zest in a small bowl. Season with salt and pepper to taste. Store in an airtight container and refrigerate for up to 1 week.

FOODS
OF A
CHAMPION

Senegalese wrestling (*laamb* in Wolof) is our national sport, even more popular than soccer. Wrestling champions are heroes in Senegal and receive hefty sums for their fights—sometimes hundreds of thousands of dollars for marquee fights. These fights, organized by promoters, are always a rowdy, high-energy spectacle attended by excited crowds rooting for their local god-like champions against a backdrop of singing and drumming. Wrestlers and their entourages perform choreographed dance moves to summon courage and intimidate their opponents while the fans' excitement and anticipation reach a fever pitch.

The star wrestlers, whose images you'll find plastered on billboards and potato chip bags alike, are built like giants. The fights, which can be very short, end when a wrestler throws his opponent to the ground. Simply dressed in loincloths similar to those of sumo wrestlers, a Senegalese wrestler strikes an intimidating figure. Since bare-fisted blows are allowed, the fights can sometimes be bloody.

Though the fights themselves can end quickly, there is a long, mystical preparation that includes elements of black magic. Indeed, although intense physical training is key, many say that a fighter is only as good as his *marabout*, a mystical man whose traditional magic helps to shield his fighter from the hexes of his opponents. There are many secret rituals even before the wrestler enters the stadium and during the fight, wrestlers wear protective talismans. Thiaw, a wrestler originally from the Saloum region, told me that "no one would dare enter the arena without mystical protection."

During the prematch singing and dancing, you might see wrestlers carrying hollowed-out calabashes from which they pour milky liquid all over themselves to bring luck in the arena. The bark of the baobab tree finds its way into some of the protective baths the *marabouts* prepare for the wrestlers. Occasionally, wrestlers in the audience dance up to another wrestler and smash a calabash on the ground, challenging him to a future fight.

Although the magical liquids the *marabouts* prepare are secret and complex, Thiaw's diet is surprisingly simple. He credits his success in the wrestling arena to his traditional diet. "I grew up eating millet and since I am from the Saloum region, that's the grain I eat most. I love it couscous-style, simply steamed with grilled fish, mollusks, or a lamb stew. My favorite dish is *thiéré mboum*, millet with *moringa* and root vegetables. In the morning, I also like fresh milk and millet. My favorite snack is fresh mango. As you see, my diet is very simple. Late nights, I enjoy an occasional *dibi*."

When asked about those who look down on healthy traditional foods and prefer imported processed foods, he said, "People forget their tradition and yet this is all we have."

Sports are a major part of the social fabric of Dakar. Every day, around late afternoon, the long stretch of Corniche Avenue along the Atlantic Ocean is crowded with people of all ages and genders jogging or working out. Around the same time, most beaches turn into soccer or wrestling arenas.

CAMEROONIAN CHICKEN
ROASTED IN KRAFT PAPER

SERVES

4

This dish was inspired by a similar one that I eat at L'Endroit, a Cameroonian restaurant in Dakar where my dear friend Chef Christian Abegan consulted on the menu. Cooking in kraft paper is a popular technique in West Africa. It reminds me of a way to prepare lamb *dibi*, in which the meat is wrapped in kraft paper with all the seasonings and slowly cooked in the back of a wood-burning oven. The concept of cooking *en papillote* is comparable. The result is flavorful, juicy, moist, and tender meat. As always, have some baguettes to mop up the juices, and *kani* sauce to give it a kick.

1 large red or yellow onion, thickly sliced

3 garlic cloves, minced

1 tablespoon peeled, minced fresh ginger

1 tablespoon chopped fresh thyme leaves

1 tablespoon Dijon mustard

1 tablespoon peanut oil or other light vegetable oil

1 tablespoon fine sea salt

1 teaspoon freshly ground black pepper

1 teaspoon cayenne pepper

2 tablespoons white vinegar

1 (3 to 4-pound) free-range chicken, cut into 8 pieces

2 tablespoons water

Baguettes, for serving

Raw Kani Sauce (recipe follows), for serving

❯❯ Combine the onion, garlic, ginger, thyme, mustard, oil, salt, black pepper, cayenne, and vinegar in a large bowl. Add the chicken pieces and combine to coat. Cover with plastic wrap and let marinate overnight in the refrigerator.

❯❯ Preheat the oven to 350°F with a rack in the center position.

❯❯ Line a baking sheet with a piece of kraft paper large enough to enclose the chicken and onions. Spread the onions in a layer in the center of the paper and place the chicken on top. Carefully pour on the marinade and water. Fold the paper tightly around the chicken and onions, enclosing them in a completely sealed package. Place the chicken on the baking sheet in the oven and bake for 1 hour and 30 minutes, until the chicken is cooked through.

❯❯ Serve the chicken and onions directly from the paper or transfer them to a platter and pour the juices over them. Have some baguettes nearby for the juices, and a side of kani sauce, too.

NOTE: *Instead of a sheet of kraft paper, you can also place the chicken inside a large, clean paper grocery bag and tie the opening closed with kitchen twine. Other options include using a double layer of parchment paper or aluminum foil, or even an ovenproof casserole with a tightly fitting lid. Be sure **not** to use wax paper.*

RAW KANI SAUCE

This raw version of the traditional *kani* sauce is a killer that will make you sweat. We call it *confiture de piment*, which translates to "pepper jam," but don't let that fool you—this incendiary sauce is not a spread for your breakfast toast. All you need is a pinch at a time on the side of a hearty dish to bring the fire you're looking for.

Makes about ¾ cup

5 Scotch bonnet peppers, coarsely chopped

½ cup diced yellow onion

2 garlic cloves, peeled

2 tablespoons Dijon mustard

1 tablespoon salt

1 teaspoon freshly ground black pepper

2 tablespoons vegetable oil

❯❯ Place all the ingredients in a blender or a mortar. Blend or pound with a pestle to create a smooth sauce. Store refrigerated in an airtight container for up to 2 weeks.

SPICY KELEWELE FRIED CHICKEN

1 cup peanut flour
(see page 68)

2 tablespoons fine sea salt

1 teaspoon ground ginger

1 teaspoon onion powder

1 teaspoon garlic powder

1 teaspoon cayenne pepper

½ teaspoon freshly ground
black pepper

1 free-range chicken (about
3 to 4 pounds), cut into 8
pieces

2 cups all-purpose flour

Peanut oil, for frying

Fried plantains or mashed
sweet potatoes, for serving

Sautéed greens, for serving

The spice mixture in this fried chicken is inspired by the Ghanaian street food *kelewele*, fried seasoned plantains. Since West African food often transcends colonial borders, I added the quintessential Senegalese peanut flour to the mix. Now this fried chicken is as Senegalese as it is Ghanaian.

⟩⟩ In a large bowl, combine the peanut flour, salt, ginger, onion powder, garlic powder, cayenne, and black pepper. Add the chicken and mix well. Cover with plastic wrap and marinate in the refrigerator overnight.

⟩⟩ Line a baking sheet or platter with several layers of paper towels. Pour oil into a large cast-iron skillet or other heavy, straight-sided pan to a depth of 1 inch, and heat to 350°F over medium-high heat.

⟩⟩ Working in batches, dredge the chicken pieces in the flour. Lightly tap the pieces to shake off the excess flour and carefully place in the hot oil. Fry the pieces for 10 to 15 minutes, turning once, until deep golden brown on all sides and cooked through. Keep the oil temperature around 350°F, adjusting the heat if too hot or cool.

⟩⟩ Remove with a slotted spoon or tongs and drain on the paper towels. Serve with fried plantains or mashed sweet potatoes and sautéed greens.

SENEGALESE SEOUL

In Dakar, most *maquis* names start with the word "Chez," followed by the name of the owner, including the popular Chez Iba and Chez Djamil. However, this rule doesn't apply to one of my favorite Dakar hangouts, Seoul 2.

How did a notorious underground sports bar and *dibiterie* joint run by a Senegalese mother-daughter team in Dakar come to be named after the capital of South Korea, when there is nothing Korean about it? It was 2002 and the World Cup was being held in Korea and Japan. That year, our beloved Senegalese soccer team, the Lions of Teranga, brilliantly reached the quarterfinals—a first-ever for an African team. They had shocked the world in their opening game by beating the then world champion, our former colonizer, France, by 1–0.

That day, the whole country was in a state of euphoria, and the courtyard restaurant felt as if it were inside the stadium in Seoul. The fans were screaming and commenting at the television screen while enjoying their grilled pork chops, lamb *dibi*, quail, Guinea hen, whole *thioff*, and fried plantains, all washed down with ice-cold Gazelle, our popular local beer. Since then, the place has been forever known as Seoul 2.

CHICKEN THIGHS

with RED PALM–COCONUT RICE

- 8 skin-on, bone-in chicken thighs (about 2 pounds total)
- Fine sea salt and freshly ground black pepper
- 2 tablespoons vegetable oil
- 1 large yellow onion, thinly sliced
- 2 garlic cloves, coarsely chopped
- 2 cups jasmine rice
- 1½ cups full-fat coconut milk
- 1½ cups chicken stock
- 2 tablespoons red palm oil or vegetable oil
- Juice of 1 lime
- 2 tablespoons chopped fresh cilantro, or more to taste
- Sautéed greens, for serving

Jenn Sit inspired this comforting one-pot dish reminiscent of our *thiebou guinaar*, also known as "the original jambalaya." I added coconut milk and red palm oil instead of just the traditional chicken stock to cook the rice. The coconut milk adds subtle flavor, nuanced by the complex hints of red palm oil. The lime juice and cilantro added just before serving bring it all together. A side of sautéed collard greens or kale completes the meal.

 » Season the chicken thighs with salt and pepper. In a large cast-iron pot or Dutch oven with a heavy lid, heat the vegetable oil over medium-high heat. When hot, working in batches if necessary, sear the chicken thighs very well, skin side first, letting the skin get a nice golden color (about 5 minutes) before turning once and browning the other side. Remove from the pot and set aside on a platter.

 » Discard all but 1 tablespoon of rendered chicken fat. Add the onions and cook, stirring frequently with a wooden spoon, until soft and slightly golden, about 5 minutes. Add the garlic and the rice and stir to coat the rice well.

Add the coconut milk and chicken stock and stir to combine. Bring to a boil, reduce the heat to a simmer, and stir in the red palm oil. Season with 1 teaspoon salt and 1 teaspoon pepper.

 » Return the chicken thighs and any juices to the pot, setting them on top of the rice, and cover. Simmer for 25 to 30 minutes, until all the liquid is absorbed, the rice is tender, and the chicken is cooked through.

 » When you're ready to serve, squeeze the lime juice all over the chicken and rice and generously top with cilantro. Serve with a side of greens.

NIGERIAN DIBI HAUSA *Suya*, known as *dibi Hausa* in Senegal, is a style of grilled skewered meat from the Hausa tribe of northern Nigeria and Niger. It was one of my favorite snacks growing up in Dakar. Unlike other styles of *dibi*, the meat in *dibi Hausa* is thinly cut into boneless pieces, then skewered and grilled over small hot charcoal stoves manned by vendors on bustling downtown Dakar street corners. Most importantly, *dibi Hausa* is sprinkled with the addictive *kan kan kan*, a dry mixture made of finely ground peanuts and spices. Served on kraft paper with thinly sliced raw onions and extra *kan kan kan* on the side, *dibi Hausa* is a must.

SUYA-SPICED
GRILLED CHICKEN LIVERS

- 1 pound chicken livers, cleaned
- 1 teaspoon salt
- 1 teaspoon freshly ground black pepper
- 1 tablespoon vegetable oil, plus more for brushing
- ½ cup Kan Kan Kan Spice Mix (page 87), plus more for dipping
- ½ cup peanut flour (see page 68)
- ½ cup thinly sliced yellow onions, for serving

Suya spices, also known as *kan kan kan*, are very popular wherever Hausa people live, which means pretty much everywhere in West Africa since they have a long tradition of intermarriage with the nomadic Fulani. The spice mix is traditionally used for beef or lamb, but it works perfectly with chicken or even fish. Chargrilled, slightly spicy, and served with raw onions for an added crunch—this is, to me, the way to go with chicken livers.

》 Soak bamboo skewers in water for at least an hour before cooking. Preheat the grill or grill pan to hot.

》 In a bowl, season the livers with salt, pepper, and oil. Add the spice mix and peanut flour and mix well. Thread the livers onto skewers to fit. Set on a platter, cover loosely with plastic wrap, and refrigerate for 30 minutes.

》 Lightly brush the livers with oil before setting them on the hot grill. Grill for 2 minutes on each side.

》 Serve hot with extra spice mix as a dry dip and the onions on the side.

GRILLED HANGER STEAK
with GREEN PAPAYA SALAD

SERVES
4

This dish, perfect for summer, has a few inspirations: First there is *abuko*, the grilled beef salad of our Gambian neighbors. Then there is my Vietnamese godfather, Uncle Jean, who taught me how to season the meat with fish sauce, ginger, garlic, and sugar. Finally, the green papaya salad that accompanies the steak is also Vietnamese-influenced, but reminiscent of the way we used to eat green mangoes as kids growing up in Senegal, simply dusted with cayenne pepper and salt.

The hanger cut is perfect for a salad when you take the time to marinate the meat—I like to start early in the day so that my meat marinates for up to 12 hours in the refrigerator. To me, medium-rare is the perfect way to eat a hanger steak, but if you are like most Senegalese and want your meat cooked all the way through, go for it.

STEAK
- **2 tablespoons peeled, minced fresh ginger**
- **1 teaspoon minced garlic**
- **2 tablespoons sugar**
- **3 tablespoons Vietnamese or Thai fish sauce**
- **1 tablespoon cayenne pepper**
- **1½ to 2 pounds hanger steak (membrane removed)**
- **Salt and freshly ground black pepper**

GREEN PAPAYA SALAD
- **¼ cup sugar**
- **¼ cup fresh lime juice**
- **1 teaspoon grated lime zest**
- **2 teaspoons cayenne pepper**
- **1 teaspoon salt**
- **1 teaspoon freshly ground black pepper**
- **½ green papaya, peeled, seeded, and finely shredded**
- **1 carrot, peeled and finely shredded**
- **1 small red onion, thinly sliced**
- **¼ cup roasted unsalted peanuts, chopped**
- **½ cup chopped fresh cilantro**

» **To prepare the steak:** In a bowl, combine the ginger, garlic, sugar, fish sauce, and cayenne. Cut the meat into four equal portions and add to the marinade. Turn to coat well. Cover tightly with plastic wrap and marinate for 12 hours in the refrigerator.

» **To prepare the salad:** Combine the sugar, lime juice, lime zest, cayenne, salt, and black pepper in a large bowl. Add the papaya, carrot, and red onion and toss well. Cover and refrigerate for 2 hours.

» When you're ready to cook, remove the hanger steak from the refrigerator and let it sit at room temperature for 30 minutes while you preheat the grill or a grill pan to hot.

» Season the steaks with salt and pepper and grill for 8 to 10 minutes for medium-rare, turning occasionally. Let the meat rest for about 5 minutes in a warm area or tented with aluminum foil. Thinly slice it on an angle, across the grain.

» Drain the papaya salad and serve with the steak, topped with the peanuts and cilantro.

SWEET THINGS

BANANA COCONUT FRITTERS

2 cups millet flour

1 cup finely shredded unsweetened coconut

½ cup granulated sugar

2 teaspoons salt

2 cups full-fat coconut milk

2 teaspoons dark rum

Vegetable oil, for frying

4 ripe bananas

Confectioners' sugar, for serving

These banana fritters are both gluten-free and delicious. Coconut trees symbolize the best of the Casamance region, where they are considered "nature's gift to the world." Indeed, every part of the tree is used here: the strong trunk as pillars for construction, the leaves for roofs or fencing, the fruit's shells as fuel in the kitchen. Even the sap serves as a sweet beverage or a fermented wine. This coconut batter can be used for other fruits as well. To be extra indulgent, serve with Hibiscus Coulis (page 278) and Coconut-Lime-Palm Ice Cream (page 293).

» In a large bowl, combine the flour, coconut, granulated sugar, salt, coconut milk, and rum. Whisk until smooth. Cover with plastic wrap and let rest for 1 hour at room temperature.

» Line a baking sheet or platter with several layers of paper towels. Pour oil into a large cast-iron skillet or other heavy, straight-sided pan to a depth of 1 inch, and heat to 350°F over medium-high heat.

» Peel the bananas and slice on an angle into ½-inch-thick pieces. One at a time, dip banana slices in the batter to coat, then gently drop into the hot oil. Do not overcrowd the pan. Fry until golden brown on both sides, 3 to 4 minutes. Remove with a slotted spoon and drain on the paper towels. Repeat until all the bananas are used.

» Serve warm, topped with confectioners' sugar.

Home-cooked beignets in Senegal: coconut beignets on the left, millet beignets on the right.

MILLET BEIGNETS
(BEIGNETS DUGUB)

Millet beignets are a street food that can be seen in many parts of West Africa. There are lots of different versions, but I like this simple sweet one with a hint of vanilla.

2 cups millet flour

1 cup all-purpose flour

1 teaspoon salt

2 large eggs

1 cup granulated sugar

¼ cup unsalted butter, melted

⅔ cup whole milk

1 vanilla bean, split lengthwise, seeds scraped

Pinch of ground nutmeg

1 (¼-ounce) packet active dry yeast

Vegetable oil, for frying

Confectioners' sugar, for serving

Hibiscus Coulis (page 278; optional)

❯❯ In a large bowl, combine the millet flour, all-purpose flour, and salt and mix well. Dig a well in the center.

❯❯ In a separate bowl, whisk together the eggs and granulated sugar until the sugar dissolves. Pour into the well in the flour, add the butter, and mix with a wooden spoon until combined.

❯❯ In a small pot, heat the milk with the vanilla bean halves, the scraped seeds, and nutmeg to a tepid temperature. Remove from the heat and stir in the yeast to dissolve it. Remove and discard the vanilla bean halves. Gradually pour the milk into the flour-egg mixture, stirring with a wooden spoon to incorporate it. The batter should be thick, not runny.

❯❯ Cover the bowl with a clean kitchen towel and let the batter rest at room temperature for about 30 minutes.

❯❯ Line a baking sheet or platter with several layers of paper towels. Pour the oil into a large, deep cast-iron skillet or other heavy pot to a depth of 2 inches, and heat to 350°F over medium-high heat.

❯❯ Drop a few generous tablespoons of batter into the hot oil (do not overcrowd). Fry until golden brown for about 2 to 3 minutes, turning frequently.

❯❯ Remove with a slotted spoon and drain on the paper towels. Repeat until all the batter is used. Serve the beignets warm or at room temperature, dusted with confectioners' sugar, with hibiscus coulis for dipping.

SENEGALESE SPOTLIGHT:

Keur Moussa Monastery, Spreading the Locavore Word

Keur Moussa Monastery, founded in 1963, is a peaceful Benedictine monastery located about an hour outside of Dakar. Our host, Brother Simon, gave us a fascinating tour of the farm and orchards on which this self-sustaining monastery survives. There were acres of trees of all kinds: cashew, grapefruit, kumquat, and black peppercorn, just to name a few. From the fruit, Brother Simon creates specialty liqueurs, spirits, wines, and nonalcoholic juices and syrups.

According to Brother Simon, "each year for four to six months, tons of various fruits—especially mangoes, grapefruits, oranges, and watermelons—flood the market, and supply far exceeds demand. The fruits are sold for immediate consumption; there is very little preserving, despite the emergence in recent years of small-scale processing units. As a result, tons of fruit rot and are thrown away, which is a significant loss of income, particularly for retailers."

The answer for Brother Simon and the monastery was to find a solution in which the huge surplus of fruit could be saved. "In a country in a constant search for food security, we couldn't remain inactive and indifferent to such waste."

The day I visited with the AfroEats group (see page 53), the monks prepared a lavish picnic lunch for us. Every single dish was a product of their farm: beautiful grilled vegetables, pork chops with mango, chicken with peppers and onions, and freshly baked loaves of bread served with an amazing cheese made from goat milk from the local Fulani herds. All of this was washed down with the monks' hibiscus wine, baobab juice, and tamarind liqueur.

Although they've achieved so much already, Brother Simon is keenly aware of the obstacles that lie ahead as they continue to expand their reach, hoping to export to Western countries: "Our products could help showcase the cultural and culinary richness of Senegal. The challenge is to ensure consistent quality. This requires experience, and that takes time. Most importantly, it takes a profound change of mentality so that the pursuit of excellence, a nonnegotiable objective, always remains within Senegalese crafts."

CHOCOLATE MANGO POUND CAKE

- ⅓ cup unsalted butter, at room temperature, plus more for greasing the pan
- 1 cup all-purpose flour
- 1 teaspoon baking soda
- 1 teaspoon baking powder
- ¼ cup honey
- ½ cup packed light brown sugar
- ½ teaspoon salt
- 1 cup finely chopped ripe mango (preferably the less-stringy champagne variety)
- ½ teaspoon vanilla extract
- 1 large egg
- ½ cup plain full-fat Greek-style yogurt
- 1 cup semisweet chocolate chips

This rich, moist mango cake is one of my favorite desserts during the rainy season in Senegal, when it seems as if mangoes are growing from every other tree, yet I can never get enough of them.

» Preheat oven to 350°F with a rack in the center position. Grease an 8½ by 4½-inch loaf pan.

» Mix together the flour, baking soda, and baking powder.

» In the bowl of a mixer, combine the butter, honey, brown sugar, and salt. Beat with the paddle attachment on medium-high speed until light, about 5 minutes. Add the mango and vanilla and beat, until just combined.

» Reduce the mixer speed to low and beat in the egg. Slowly beat in the flour mixture; stop mixing as soon as it's combined. Add the yogurt and mix just until it's incorporated, about 5 seconds. Fold in the chocolate chips with a rubber spatula.

» Transfer the batter to the prepared loaf pan. Bake on the center rack for 45 minutes or until a toothpick inserted in the center comes out clean.

» Cool the cake in the pan on a rack and serve.

RED PALM BROWNIES

1 cup red palm oil or unsalted butter, plus more for greasing the pan

2 cups granulated sugar

4 large eggs

2 teaspoons vanilla extract

²/₃ cup unsweetened cocoa powder

1 cup all-purpose flour

1 teaspoon ground selim pepper

¼ teaspoon cayenne pepper

½ teaspoon baking powder

½ teaspoon kosher salt

Confectioners' sugar or ice cream, for serving

Using the same selim pepper that makes café Touba so unique, these brownies quickly become addictive, especially if you are patient enough to let them sit overnight, allowing the spices to slowly permeate the brownies. They go wonderfully well with ice cream, which has a soothing effect on the heat of the spices.

» Preheat the oven to 350°F. Line a 9 by 13-inch baking dish with parchment paper, leaving an overhang at the ends. Lightly grease the paper.

» In a bowl, combine the palm oil, granulated sugar, eggs, and vanilla and whisk until well combined. Add the cocoa, flour, selim pepper, cayenne, baking powder, and salt and mix until smooth.

» Spread the batter in the prepared baking dish. Bake until a toothpick inserted in the middle comes out fudgy, 20 to 25 minutes.

» Cool in the baking dish on a rack. Use the parchment paper to lift the brownies out of the pan before slicing. Serve simply dusted with confectioners' sugar or with ice cream.

GUAVA-STUFFED FRENCH TOAST
(MBURU FASS)

SERVES 4

Mburu fass is a treat we loved as kids in Senegal. It was Mom's way of using up stale bread. Unlike the original recipe, I sandwich the bread with guava jam and dip it in a vanilla-infused egg batter. French toast prepared this way has so much more character. You can serve it as is, or with Hibiscus Coulis (page 278) or fresh fruit.

- ½ cup unsalted butter, at room temperature, plus more for cooking
- 1 teaspoon grated lime zest
- 1 stale baguette, cut into ½-inch-thick slices (about 24 slices)
- ½ cup guava jam
- 2 large eggs, slightly beaten
- 1 cup sweetened condensed milk
- ½ cup whole milk
- Seeds scraped from 1 vanilla bean
- Confectioners' sugar, for serving

» In a small bowl, combine the butter and lime zest. Evenly spread half of the baguette slices on one side with 2 teaspoons of the butter each. Spread each of the remaining slices on one side with 2 teaspoons jam. Make sandwiches with the buttered and guava slices.

» In a shallow pan or bowl, combine the eggs, condensed milk, whole milk, and vanilla seeds and mix well. Dip the sandwiches into this batter until well coated on both sides.

» Heat a large nonstick frying pan over medium heat and add a pat of butter. When the butter is hot, add the sandwiches in batches and cook until golden brown on both sides, 3 to 4 minutes per side.

» Serve warm, sprinkled with confectioners' sugar.

HIBISCUS BRÛLÉE TART

with RED PALM OIL CRUST

Dessert is not really a Senegalese tradition; we usually snack on fruits and other sweets at different times of the day. For this dessert, however, I used French baking techniques and Senegalese ingredients. The crust is made with red palm oil instead of butter and the filling is a striking dark hibiscus custard. It's finished with a thin layer of caramelized sugar, which you can omit if you do not have a torch.

◉

» To prepare the crust: Whisk together the confectioners' sugar and egg yolks in a large bowl. In a separate bowl, rubbing with your hands, combine the flour, oil, and salt until the texture resembles cornmeal. Add the vanilla seeds, lime zest, and yolk-sugar mixture and combine with a wooden spoon until the dough holds together.

» On a large piece of plastic wrap, mold the dough into a rectangle. Wrap it in plastic wrap and refrigerate for 1 hour. Roll the dough onto floured parchment paper into a thin disk, ⅛-inch thick and 10 to 12 inches in diameter. Place on a baking sheet and freeze for 30 minutes.

» Preheat the oven to 350°F.

» Line an 8-inch round tart pan with the cold dough, trimming off the excess. Using a fork, prick the bottom of the crust. Freeze once more for 10 minutes.

» Blind bake the crust: Line the crust with parchment paper and use dried beans as weight. Bake for 15 minutes.

» Remove the paper and beans and bake for another 10 minutes, until lightly browned. Remove from the oven and set aside to cool to room temperature. Reduce the oven temperature to 250°F.

» To prepare the filling: In a large heatproof bowl, whisk together the eggs, egg yolk, and granulated sugar until pale and thick. Very slowly whisk in the hibiscus infusion until well combined. Fill a saucepan with water, bring to a boil, then reduce to a simmer over low heat. Place the bowl on top and using a heatproof rubber spatula, constantly stir the custard until it thickens and reaches 160°F.

» Strain the custard through a fine-mesh sieve into the crust. Spread it evenly with the spatula. Bake for 25 to 30 minutes, until a toothpick stuck in the center of the filling comes out clean. Remove from the oven and set aside to cool.

» While the tart bakes, prepare the sugared hibiscus: Bring the simple syrup to a boil and add the hibiscus. Cook until the syrup thickens and coats the hibiscus. Drain the hibiscus and set aside to cool slightly.

» If you have a kitchen blowtorch, sprinkle a very thin layer of golden sugar on the surface of the tart. Caramelize it with the torch. Arrange the sugared hibiscus atop the tart in a decorative fashion. Serve as is or with ice cream.

CRUST

½ **cup confectioners' sugar**

3 **large egg yolks**

1¼ **cups all-purpose flour**

½ **cup red palm oil or cold unsalted butter**

1 **teaspoon fine sea salt**

Seeds scraped from 1 vanilla bean

Grated zest of 2 limes

HIBISCUS FILLING

9 **large whole eggs**

1 **large egg yolk**

1½ **cups granulated sugar**

1½ **cups Hibiscus Infusion (page 284)**

SUGARED HIBISCUS

1 **cup simple syrup (see Note)**

12 **whole dried red hibiscus flowers**

Unrefined golden sugar (optional)

Ice cream, for serving (optional)

NOTE: *Simple syrup is indeed simple to make. Combine equal volumes of water and sugar in a saucepan and bring to a boil. Simmer for a few minutes until the sugar dissolves. If not using immediately in the recipe, let it cool and store in a jar in the refrigerator for up to a month.*

SWEET HIBISCUS PLANTAINS

6 firm, ripe plantains (still yellow), peels on

Hibiscus Coulis (recipe follows) or maple syrup

This recipe was inspired by a grilled plantain dish my good friend Alpha Toure serves at his hotel, Le Coral Beach, in Grand Bassam, Côte d'Ivoire. He jokingly calls the dish "Croissant Bété" after the Bété people who are supposedly very fond of it. Instead of using the traditional green plantain, this version uses sweet, ripened plantains that are grilled first and finished in the oven with a hibiscus coulis. I used to serve this dish at my restaurant for brunch with a side of eggs, and in this light, I'd suggest that maple syrup would make an easy substitute for the hibiscus coulis. In addition to breakfast, these plantains would make a great side to grilled fish or meat, or just eaten as a snack.

》 Preheat a grill to medium heat, and preheat the oven to 375°F.

》 Grill the plantains with the peels on for about 15 minutes, until lightly charred. Remove from the grill and carefully peel. Brush each plantain with the coulis and place on a lightly oiled baking sheet.

》 Bake the glazed plantains for about 5 minutes, until golden brown. Let cool and serve.

HIBISCUS COULIS

Makes ½ cup

¼ cup dried red hibiscus flowers
1 cup water
1 cup granulated sugar

》 In a small saucepan, combine the hibiscus, water, and sugar. Bring to a boil and reduce to a thick syrup, about 10 minutes. Place the mixture in a food processor or blender and purée. Strain through a fine sieve, discard the solids, and use chilled (it will thicken as it chills).

SWEET POTATO-MANGO SPICE CAKE

Sweet potato and mango—two of my favorite ingredients—is a marriage that works, and so it is with cinnamon and ginger. They all come together in this fortunate love affair: a warm spice cake that would be even more excellent finished with a dollop of freshly whipped cream and served with hot tea.

⊙

» Preheat the oven to 325°F. Lightly grease a 10-inch round cake pan.

» In a large bowl, combine the flour, cinnamon, ginger, baking soda, and salt. In another bowl, combine the sweet potato, mango, sugar, and oil. Beat with an electric mixer until smooth. Add the eggs one at a time while still beating. Add the vanilla and mix briefly. Add the flour mixture and beat until just blended.

» Pour the batter into the prepared pan. Bake until a toothpick inserted in the center comes out clean, about 1 hour.

» Cool completely in the pan on a rack, then turn onto a plate and serve.

1 cup vegetable oil, plus more for greasing the pan

2¾ cups all-purpose flour

2 teaspoons ground cinnamon

2 teaspoons ground ginger

1 teaspoon baking soda

1 teaspoon salt

1 cup mashed roasted sweet potato

1 cup finely chopped mango

2 cups sugar

4 large eggs

1 teaspoon vanilla extract

HERDERS WITHOUT BORDERS

"Eat that you may live, not that you may fatten"

(Niam n'goura vana niam m'paya)

—FULANI PROVERB

The Fulani people, whose origins stem from the interaction between West Africans and the Berber people of North Africa, comprise the largest nomadic group of people in the world today. Fulanis herd cattle, goats, and sheep; the more heads you own, the higher you are in society. When the time comes to move to greener pasture, they take down their temporary housing to rebuild on their new land. Nowadays, many Fulani have settled and abandoned the nomadic life; some are even farming, which was once considered a rejection of ancestral traditions. This change in lifestyle has also influenced their diet, which traditionally consisted of products from the herd along with nuts and fruits gathered from the wild, but now includes millet, corn, rice, and cassava.

Kossam, as milk is called in Fulbe (the Fulani language), is venerated and consumed fresh or made into yogurt, cheese, and butter (*kettugol*). Fulanis mostly trade in fresh and sour milk, and sell their cattle only when the need arises. One of the most popular meals in Senegal is the Fulani *latchiiri* or *dakkere*, also called *lakh* in Wolof. Traditionally served at naming ceremonies, *latchiiri* consists of fermented milk (yogurt) and corn or millet couscous.

Paradoxically, the Fulani diet consists of little meat, as they place more value on milk. Consequently, cows are the most prized among the herd. Many Fulanis also do not eat goat meat, which they superstitiously connect with leprosy. They drink goat milk, but they wouldn't feed it to their infants. The delicious cheese from the Keur Moussa Monastery (see page 268) is made with goat milk collected from local Fulani herders.

As in most parts of Africa, food is the domain of nurturing women. In addition to cooking and market shopping, they milk the cows and churn the milk for butter. At local markets, you'll see women with decorated calabashes balanced atop their heads from which they sell yogurt, cheese, and butter.

SENEGALESE SPOTLIGHT:
La Laiterie du Berger

Bagoré Bathily, a Senegalese veterinarian and entrepreneur, couldn't understand why 90 percent of the milk sold in Senegal was imported while herding is the sole means of subsistence for 30 percent of the Senegalese population. Thus, he started La Laiterie du Berger, a company that produces yogurt or *lait caillé* (milk curds) from milk bought from local herders.

One of his main motivations was to ensure a regular income for the herders, and he has established a relationship based on trust with them. His veterinarian background is also put to good use as he raises awareness amongst the herders on topics such as animal hygiene and nutrition. When the dry season comes, he supplies the herders with feed (rice bran and groundnuts); otherwise the herds would leave in search of pasture and the Laiterie would be without milk. Dr. Bathily built the yogurt processing facilities in 2006 near the Senegal River Delta in the town of Richard Toll. Since then, the business has grown rapidly, and by 2012 he was selling close to 4,000 liters of yogurt per day.

GINGER-HIBISCUS
POACHED MANGOES

2 green mangoes, peeled
2 cups ginger juice (see Note)
2 cups Hibiscus Infusion
   (recipe follows)

NOTE: *Making your own ginger juice is very easy. Combine a ¼ pound of peeled, chopped ginger in a blender with ½ cup of water and purée. Strain well and dilute with 1½ cups more water. Adjust to taste with lime, honey, and more water if it's too strong.*

This recipe was inspired by the classic dessert of pears poached in red wine. Here green mangoes are poached in a ginger-hibiscus infusion. You could use ripe mangoes instead, but I find poached green mangoes more intriguing to the palate. The acidity of the mango seems to evolve as it gently simmers in the ginger-hibiscus infusion, balancing the sweetness and spiciness. The poached mangoes are delicious served as is, or alongside the Chocolate Mango Pound Cake (page 272) or the Spicy Café Touba Brownies (page 274).

» Cut the cheeks of mango flesh from the sides of the pits and halve them lengthwise.

» In a large saucepan, combine the ginger juice and hibiscus infusion. Heat over medium heat until warm. Gently add the mango pieces and simmer over low heat for 15 minutes, until the mango is soft. Remove from the heat and let the mangoes cool in the poaching liquid.

» Once slightly cooled, thinly slice the mango lengthwise and spread in a fan in serving bowls. Bring the poaching liquid to a boil over high heat and cook for 10 to 15 minutes, until syrupy. Spoon the hot syrup over the mango slices and serve warm.

HIBISCUS INFUSION

Makes 1 quart

2 cups dried red hibiscus flowers
1 quart water
Sugar or honey (optional, if drinking as a beverage)

» Combine the hibiscus and water in a saucepan and bring to a boil. Remove from the heat and set aside to cool.

» Strain well and discard the hibiscus. If enjoying as a beverage, not as part of a recipe, add sugar or honey to taste. Store in an airtight container in the refrigerator for up to 1 week.

BAOBAB
FRUIT GRANITA

This is a really fresh and easy way to enjoy baobab in the summer. It can be served over a fruit salad or just as is.

2 cups water
1 cup sugar
3 cups Baobab Fruit Drink
(page 308)

◉

» Combine the water and sugar in a saucepan and bring to a boil. Reduce the heat to a simmer, and cook, stirring, until the sugar dissolves. Remove from the heat and let cool completely.

» Add the baobab drink and mix well. Pour into a large metal bowl or shallow baking pan and place in the freezer. Every 30 minutes, whisk and scrape with a fork. After 2 hours, transfer to a container with a tight lid and freeze for another hour before serving.

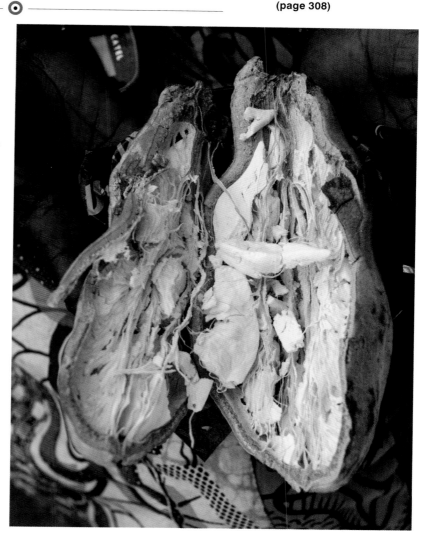

THE WOMEN OF SENEGAL: MY INSPIRATION

Naked woman, black woman
Clothed with your color, which is life, with your form, which is beauty
In your shadow I have grown up; the softness of your hands
    shielded my eyes
And now at the height of Summer and Noon,
From the crest of charred hilltops, I discover you, Promised Land
And your beauty strikes my heart like an eagle's lightning flash.

— An excerpt from "Black Woman," a poem by **LÉOPOLD SÉDAR SENGHOR**, Senegal's first president. It is a hymn to Senegalese women, in which the "black woman" is often interpreted as a metaphor for the nation of Senegal.

Due to chronic unemployment of the men, Senegalese women are quite often the main source of revenue for their families. They have an entrepreneurial spirit and are frequently engaged in some sort of trade or commerce. In addition to handling all the food shopping and cooking for their own households, you'll find Senegalese women selling goods in the markets; hawking roasted peanuts, fried beignets, or other food specialties from a humble stall in the streets; or buying seafood fresh off the boat to clean, smoke, ferment, or salt before selling locally or exporting to neighboring countries. They're also seen crisscrossing the world's major cities from Rome and Paris to Dubai, New York, and Hong Kong, trading all sorts of merchandise such as jewelry, fabrics, and condiments. Whether at home or abroad, Senegalese women are at the heart of the economic development of Senegal.

Reputed for their beauty and sense of fashion, they manage to sustain the balancing act of elegance and hard work. I am particularly impressed by their personal stories and fighting spirit in spite of adversity. In a climate of economic crisis, they often face challenges head on with patience, thoughtful planning, resilience, and dignity, while men may seem at a loss. Needless to say, they have been an inspiration to me at every step of my life.

My mom, who was also my best friend, set the standard early. She was a midwife who tirelessly worked at Le Dantec Hospital in downtown Dakar. She gave me a passion for food and for reading, which I took along for my life's journey.

Aline Sitoé, after whom my daughter is named, is a national heroine in Senegal. Born with handicapped legs, she courageously led men into resistance against the French colonial power. She refused to allow the French army to tax the Diola people's rice for their army's war effort. She was subsequently arrested and deported to Timbuktu, and never returned to Senegal again.

There are countless examples of inspiring Senegalese women, particularly in the agricultural industry, where a majority of the small businesses are women-owned.

Among them is **Aissatou Diagne Deme,** whose visionary supermarket only sells organic African products, and **Professor Saly Wade,** the founder of La Maison du Bien Manger, an organization with the goal of educating people on nutritious diets using local ingredients. There is **Chef Mawa Hugues,** who moved to Senegal after a lengthy stay in North Carolina and now runs a unique and original African- and American-style restaurant in Dakar; **Valerie Ndiaye,** the cofounder of Esteval (see page 310), a growing organic local juice company; and **Randa Filfili**, though of Lebanese descent, is as Senegalese as it gets. Her father-in-law, Mr. Toufic Filfili, was born in Guinguineo, a city in the center of Senegal, and started a farm and supermarket that became one of the leading ones in Senegal. Randa is now the head of the company, and also launched Zena Exotic Fruits, a pioneer in developing a line of natural spreads and jams of top-notch quality, bursting with Senegalese flavors. **Rokhaya Daba Gning** and **Bineta Diallo** are two female chefs who decided to start a cooking school for girls only. Their goal is to recruit the students among the neediest, and train and coach them to create small restaurants that will serve local cuisine. United States–based **Magatte Wade**, a serial entrepreneur extraordinaire, successfully started Adina World Beat Beverages, a line of juices that includes Senegalese products such as hibiscus and baobab. She now owns Tiossan, a natural skin care company that also uses local Senegalese ingredients. Magatte recently made the list of Forbes Magazine's "20 Youngest Power Women in Africa."

Last but not least, my cousin **Mylene Gomis Girardet**, whose Vietnamese father, Jean, is the first man I ever saw cooking while I was growing up in Senegal. Mylene started an original line of food containers and is working on packaging the Pink Lake's salt (see page 222).

SENEGALESE
POPSICLES

Popsicles are popular in Senegal for obvious reasons: they are easy to make and our year-round hot and sunny weather is always right for these icy treats. There is not much fussing with the preparation, as our popsicles are straight-up natural juices frozen in small plastic bags, the most common flavors being baobab fruit, hibiscus, and tamarind (things that grow in our backyard). Here I have a few super simple popsicle recipes based on some essential Senegalese flavors.

BAOBAB-COCONUT POPSICLES

Baobab fruit and coconut, both smooth and creamy, were destined to meet for this healthy, delicious ice pop. My son Haroun can definitely attest to this recipe being a winner.

Makes 8 popsicles

1 cup full-fat coconut milk
½ cup sugar
¼ teaspoon salt
1½ cups Baobab Fruit Drink (page 308)
¼ cup finely shredded unsweetened coconut

» Combine the coconut milk, sugar, and salt in a saucepan over medium heat. Stir well until the sugar dissolves, about 5 minutes.

» Transfer to a large bowl and stir in the baobab drink. Mix in the shredded coconut and set aside to cool completely.

» Stir, then divide among eight popsicle molds and insert the sticks. Freeze until hard and serve cold.

HIBISCUS POPSICLES

Popsicles sold frozen in small plastic bags used to be a treat for us during hot days in Senegal. We would simply make a tiny hole with our teeth at one corner of the bag and enjoy sucking through the frozen juice.

Makes 8 popsicles

3 cups Hibiscus Infusion (page 284), unsweetened
½ cup sugar
½ cup fresh mint leaves

» Combine all the ingredients in a saucepan over medium heat. Cook, stirring, until the sugar dissolves. Remove from the heat and set aside to cool and infuse for 10 minutes. Strain out and discard the mint leaves and let the liquid cool completely.

» Divide among eight popsicle molds and insert the sticks. Freeze until hard and serve cold.

(recipe continues)

CREAMY BAOBAB-PEANUT POPSICLES (NGALAKH)

Ngalakh is a special sweet and tangy millet couscous dish made with baobab fruit and peanut butter. It is traditionally prepared by Senegalese Christians on Good Friday and shared with Muslim neighbors. Here, I serve it frozen for a rich and creamy treat.

Makes 8 popsicles

1 cup coarse millet couscous (*thiakry*-sized; see Note)
1 cup Baobab Fruit Drink (page 308)
1 cup smooth unsweetened peanut butter or cashew butter
½ cup honey

» Wash the millet several times in a bowl until the water runs clear. Drain well. Place the millet in the top of a steamer basket lined with cheesecloth. Set over salted boiling water, cover, and steam for about 15 minutes or until tender and cooked through. Let cool.

» In a large bowl, combine the baobab drink with the peanut butter and mix well. Add the cooled millet and honey and mix until smooth. Refrigerate until cold.

» Stir, then divide the mixture among eight popsicle molds and insert the sticks. Freeze until hard and serve cold.

NOTE: *If you can't find millet couscous, use instant couscous instead and follow the cooking directions on the package. I like to add a little butter or oil while cooking to prevent the grains from sticking.*

COCONUT-LIME-PALM
ICE CREAM

SERVES
4

T his Senegalese-inspired creation has become one of my favorite ice
creams. The flavors of red palm, coconut, and lime simply work together.
It feels so rich that it is hard to believe that this ice cream has no dairy. The
taste is otherworldly and would convert anyone into a red palm oil addict.

2 cups full-fat coconut milk
½ teaspoon salt
3 tablespoons grated lime zest
1 teaspoon orange flower water
4 large egg yolks
⅔ cup sugar
¾ cup red palm oil

» In a saucepan, combine the coconut milk, salt, lime zest, and orange flower water. Cook over medium heat until barely boiling, about 5 minutes. Set aside to cool.

» In an electric mixer fitted with a whisk attachment, beat the egg yolks and sugar on medium-high speed for 3 to 5 minutes, until pale and thick. Reduce the speed to low and slowly beat in the palm oil until blended, about 2 minutes.

» Over medium heat, bring the coconut milk mixture back to a simmer. With the mixer on medium speed, slowly add the coconut milk and mix until well blended. Pour the custard back into the saucepan. Cook over medium heat, stirring constantly with a heatproof rubber spatula, until the custard is thick enough to coat the back of the spatula, about 5 minutes.

» Strain the custard through a fine-mesh sieve into a large bowl. Set aside until completely cool.

» Pour the custard into an ice cream maker and process according to the manufacturer's instructions. Scrape into a container with a tightly fitting lid and store in the freezer for up to 3 days.

Flag
Spéciale

Chez SAM

DRINKS

CAFÉ TOUBA

¼ cup green (unroasted)
   coffee beans

5 selim pepper pods, crushed,
   seeds discarded

1 teaspoon whole cloves

3 cups boiling water

Sugar

Until the economic crisis that hit Senegal in 2009, café Touba was limited to gatherings of the Mouride Sufi Brotherhood and their holy city of Touba. When hard times hit, it became evident that consuming local was the way to go, so sweet and spicy café Touba, cheaper and tastier than insipid imported Nescafé, became popular in Senegal. Though affordable, I find that the café Touba sold on the street too sweet for my taste, so I prefer to make my own.

◉

❱❱ In a small, dry frying pan, toast the coffee beans, selim pepper, and cloves, stirring frequently, until they turn a nice dark brown. Let cool.

❱❱ Finely grind the mix in a coffee grinder and place in a filter in the cone of a drip coffee maker. Slowly pour the boiling water over the blend and let it drip into two mugs. Sweeten to taste and serve hot.

Café Touba, the sacred coffee drink, is named after the holy city of Touba where it was first served at religious gatherings to keep devotees awake during night prayers. During the economic recession of 2009, the *goorgorlu* (the "average Joe") could no longer afford imported coffee and turned to the local beverage more regularly. Its popularity has stuck. In fact, it has now become so popular that sellers are visible on every corner, competing with the stands that sell Nescafé's ubiquitous instant coffee.

What makes café Touba so special is its spice blend of *selim* pepper (*djar*) and cloves. Ground with coffee beans that are roasted right at the market, the combination is intoxicating. *Selim* pepper (see page 69) is a spicy African pepper that originates from Guinea and is said to have medicinal as well as aphrodisiac properties. Always served black, café Touba's highly aromatic flavor is very intense, strong, and spicy.

Most café Touba vendors walk around the streets with a pot on a stove with securely fastened plastic mugs hanging from a rope, and a bottle of sugar. They usually hang around crowded avenues where eager clients in need of a quick caffeine fix hail them down for 2- to 3-ounce shots costing only 50 CFA (less than 25 cents USD).

Ousmane, a tall and handsome young Senegalese who dresses in the colorful patchwork clothing of the Baye Fall, a subgroup of the Mouride Brotherhood, sells the popular drink, but he operates a little differently. Instead of wandering the streets of Dakar in search of customers, he sells his café Touba from a tiny kiosk amid the high-rises of downtown Dakar's Plateau area. Every morning, he purchases the freshly roasted beans at Marché HLM for approximately 1,500 CFA a kilogram (about $1.35 USD per pound). "Sometimes I make up to 10,000 CFA a day. It's a good business and everyone is doing it now," he told me. Ousmane doesn't believe in idleness. As a *mouride talibé* (faithful), his work is a form of prayer. He appeals to the jobless youths to roll up their sleeves and follow his steps.

Since Senegal doesn't produce coffee domestically, the beans are imported from Côte d'Ivoire and Guinea. Interestingly, there is now a small but growing reverse trade of the café Touba blend to our neighboring countries. In Guinea-Bissau, for instance, it has become the leading coffee beverage.

The success of café Touba is certainly linked to its connection to the holy city of Touba. Legend has it that Cheikh Amadou Bamba, the venerated Sufi mystic and founder of the city, invented it while in exile in Gabon. Bamba created the Mouride Brotherhood during the colonial occupation of Senegal by the French in the late nineteenth century. His growing popularity so worried the colonial administration that he was exiled to Gabon in 1895. When he returned from exile seven years later, his popularity grew, and today, the Mourides represent one of the strongest Sufi communities of Senegal. Café Touba is now a symbol of identity and belonging for the Senegalese community.

MINT-HIBISCUS COOLER

Also known as roselle, hibiscus is native to West Africa, and hibiscus water is one of Senegal's most popular beverages. Through the slave trade, it arrived in places like Mexico and Jamaica, where it quickly became very popular. Today, Senegal remains among the world's largest producers of hibiscus. With very high levels of antioxidants, hibiscus is healthy and in this simple recipe, refreshing. The mint infusion makes it the perfect summer drink.

1 quart plus 2 cups water

¼ **pound dried red hibiscus flowers**

¼ **cup fresh mint leaves, plus extra sprigs for garnish**

½ **cup honey or sugar**

» In a saucepan, bring 2 cups of the water, the hibiscus flowers, and mint to a boil. Turn off the heat, stir in the honey, and let cool.

» Add the remaining 1 quart water. Set aside to infuse for 10 to 15 minutes. Strain into a pitcher and refrigerate. Serve cold over ice, garnished with extra mint.

NOTE: *With the addition of light rum, this recipe makes a wonderful punch for a summer BBQ. Serve in a pitcher full of ice with a bit of rum, extra mint, and fresh lime slices.*

TAMARIND JUICE

5 cups boiling water
1 cup tamarind pulp
½ cup sugar, or more to taste

I first met friend and colleague, scholar Dr. Marco Hernandez in Dakar at the World Festival of Black Arts and Culture in 2010. Marco, who is also a chef, has written extensively on the African roots of Mexican cuisine, tracing the history of Mexico's beef culture and rice cultivation to the waves of Fulani, Mandingo, and Wolof people who were forcefully brought to the Americas in the early sixteenth century. Of course, the gastronomic influence goes both ways, as Marco points out: "Imagine: Peanuts, chocolate, tomatoes, avocados, potatoes, corn, papayas, pineapple, chile peppers, and more went from the Americas to West Africa and beyond."

Marco is especially fascinated by the West African origins of two of Mexico's most beloved "national drinks": *agua de jamaica* (hibiscus) and *agua de tamarindo* (tamarind). Wildly popular in Mexico, he was delighted to see these refreshing drinks sold everywhere in Dakar, and to discover that *dakhar* is in fact the Wolof name for tamarind. Sweet-and-sour and refreshing in both Senegalese and Mexican climes alike, try it for yourself to see what the fuss is all about.

◉

» Combine the boiling water and tamarind in a heatproof bowl and let stand 10 minutes to soften. With a wooden spoon or your fingers, break the tamarind into small pieces. Let stand 5 minutes more. Pour the mixture through a coarse strainer set over another bowl and press with the spoon to squeeze the liquid from the seeds and fibers. Discard the seeds and fibers. Add sugar and mix well. Refrigerate until cold. Serve over ice.

TAMARIND MOJITO

SERVES
2

I n 2012, I participated in *Proyecto Paladar*, an art project designed for the 11th Havana Biennial that brought U.S.-based chefs to Havana to cook with Cuban *paladar* chefs in a pop-up style restaurant made of shipping containers. In the use of fresh produce such as *moringa*, hibiscus, and tamarind, it was exciting to see firsthand how West Africa was intertwined with Spanish, Creole, and native tropical influences in Cuba's cuisine. We drank in what was said to be Hemingway's favorite bar in Havana, and supposedly his favorite drink was a mojito with tamarind, a favorite ingredient of Latin Americans and Senegalese alike.

Crushed ice

2 sprigs mint, plus more for garnish

Lime wedges

½ cup white rum

3 tablespoons Tamarind Simple Syrup (recipe follows)

2 tablespoons fresh lime juice

Club soda

⟩⟩ Fill two glasses with crushed ice. In a cocktail shaker, muddle the mint with a few lime wedges. Add the rum, tamarind syrup, lime juice, and some ice and shake vigorously. Strain into the glasses. Top with a little club soda and garnish with extra mint.

TAMARIND SIMPLE SYRUP

Makes about 1½ cups

½ cup tamarind pulp or paste
1 cup sugar
1½ cups water

⟩⟩ Combine all the ingredients in a small saucepan and bring to a boil. Cook for 1 minute, whisking, until the sugar has dissolved. Remove from the heat and set aside to cool.

⟩⟩ Strain well through a fine-mesh sieve. Store in a jar in the refrigerator for up to 3 weeks. Stir well to recombine before using.

LOCAL LIBATIONS

Although Senegal is a country with a large Muslim majority, Senegalese people are very proud of their secular constitution. Alcohol consumption is permitted and there is a flourishing nightlife scene in Dakar where bars and nightclubs compete with *maquis*, the underground watering holes that seem to exist in every neighborhood. They are extensions of homes, transformed into bars or dance venues, reminiscent of Cuban *paladares*, only with a Senegalese twist. The ambiance is always fun and the local beer flows profusely.

The oldest industrial brewery, SOBOA (Société des Brasseries de l'Ouest Africain), has been in Dakar since the late 1920s. SOBOA produces a number of pale lagers such as Flag and Castel, but the most popular by far is Gazelle. The ubiquitous Gazelle, called *Ordinaire* (meaning "ordinary") by loyalists, is the libation of choice at popular gatherings. Light, fizzy, and cheap, expect to see Gazelle's green bottle and iconic label everywhere.

There is also a thriving artisanal alcohol industry, located mostly in the Casamance and Sine Saloum regions, producing palm wine (*seung*, *bounouk*), cashew pulp liquor (*soum soum*, *cana*), and lastly, honey wine or mead (*hydromel*), a fermented mixture of water and honey that Pa Sagna, a maternal grand-uncle of mine, prepared with the wild honey he collected for his business.

PALM WINE, "THE REAL WHITE WINE"

Palm wine is a fermented drink made from the sap of the raffia palm tree. In Senegal, it is mostly consumed in the Casamance and Sine Saloum regions. Because of its milky white color, palm wine is sometimes nicknamed "the real white wine." The level of alcohol varies from one bottle to another.

Bernard Bassene, a palm wine producer from the village of Etafoune, collects sap to ferment into palm wine by climbing to the top of raffia palm trees growing around his property. Tapping palm trees for sap is a skill that requires much agility, as palm trees can grow as tall as fifty feet. To climb the trees, Bernard uses a special belt made from palm leaf fiber with twisted, knotted ends. He first passes the belt around the trunk and his waist and ties the belt's ends together. He then puts both feet on the trunk and gradually raises the belt, moving upward with his feet until he reaches the top. Bernard carries a well-worn woven bag on his shoulder in which he keeps his tools: a sharp knife and a bottle or dried gourd attached to a tiny funnel made from a palm leaf.

Once at the top, Bernard uses his knife to make an incision right below the palm tree's flower bunch, where the flow is best. It must be an incision of a specific depth, neither too deep nor too shallow. Next, he places the tiny funnel in the incision to direct the flow of sap into the attached bottle. He will return the following day to collect the filled bottles and replace them with empty ones. Though it starts to ferment from the moment it leaves the tree due to its natural yeasts, the fresh sap is very sweet and can be consumed right away as *thionkom*, a nonalcoholic beverage that kids love.

Several hours after its collection, foam begins to form inside the bottle as the sugar turns into alcohol. The length of the fermentation process will determine how strong the wine will be. It will continue to ferment if it's not refrigerated, and soon will taste sour. *Bounouk*, as it's called in Casamance, is a rather refreshing drink that pairs well with local bites such as lemony *caldou* fish, briny oysters, and spicy marinated shrimp.

My mom's village of Brin is reputed to make the best palm wine in the region. Known as *Le Bleu de Brin* because of its bluish hue, it is pleasantly sweet yet strong and refreshing with a woody flavor. It is the drink of choice for ritual ceremonies, weddings, initiations, or any traditional celebration that requires a libation in Casamance.

CASHEW WINE AND LIQUOR

In Casamance and Guinea-Bissau, *biñu di caju* ("cashew wine" in Portuguese) is a famous local drink prepared by fermenting the pulp of cashew fruits. The quickly fermenting wine is made by pressing the fruit for its juice. The pressed pulp is then given to the animals for feed or used as fertilizer. The artisanal wine is consumed locally or distilled into the strong liquor called *cana*.

Cana is a strong, clear alcohol reminiscent of tequila. This specialty of the Diola, Manjack, and Mancagne ethnicities drove the primary demand for cashew trees in the region before Indian traders, who have had offices in Ziguinchor for almost two decades now, arrived and put the focus on the cashew nut business. In Casamance, the liquor is sometimes called *soum soum*, which is not to be confused with another alcoholic drink made in the Sine Saloum region called by the same name. This other drink is prepared clandestinely with only water, sugar, and yeast (no cashews) and can be quite lethal.

» *To Our Ancestors*

The ancient tradition of pouring alcohol for our ancestors directly on the ground before drinking is a beautiful custom found everywhere in Africa. By symbolically sharing our drink with our ancestors, they remain present in our lives, and we keep our roots alive. We pour to honor the past so we may learn from it. It's another way to say grace in the spirit of remembrance.

BAOBAB
FRUIT DRINK

2½ cups baobab fruit pulp
5 cups warm water
1 tablespoon sugar

Tropical and creamy, this is one of our traditional drinks made of rehydrated baobab fruit pulp. It's very simple to make and is a great base for any number of fruit juices and smoothies.

❱❱ In a large bowl, combine all the ingredients. Stir well until the water becomes white and thick. Strain the juice into a pitcher through a fine-mesh sieve lined with damp cheesecloth. Serve chilled.

GINGER, WATERMELON & GRAPEFRUIT
JUICE

SERVES
6

½ pound fresh ginger, peeled and coarsely chopped
2 cups chopped seeded watermelon
1 quart purified water
Juice of 2 grapefruits
½ cup honey or sugar

Grandma used to always recommend ginger as a cure for flu or fatigue. Fresh and hot, it adds a zing to any drink. This one has a beautiful red hue from the sweet watermelon and complex layers of flavor from the spicy ginger and slightly bitter grapefruit. Mix in some Champagne and you'll have the perfect brunch drink.

❱❱ In a blender, combine the ginger, watermelon, and 1 cup of the water and process until puréed.

❱❱ Strain through a fine-mesh sieve lined with damp cheesecloth into a pitcher. Discard the fibers.

Add the remaining 3 cups water, the grapefruit juice, and honey.

❱❱ Taste and adjust with more water or honey if the drink is too strong for your taste. Serve cold.

GREEN CASAMANCE
SMOOTHIE

SERVES
4

The ingredients in this green smoothie are considered among the healthiest foods available in Senegal. Simply combine *moringa* leaves with coconut milk, baobab fruit juice, and your favorite fruits. In this recipe, I've chosen mango, pineapple, and avocado, all fruits that grow in the Casamance region. Green smoothies are perfect for a quick and easy energy boost, especially in the morning or afternoon.

» Pack the moringa in a blender. Add the coconut milk and baobab drink and blend until smooth, about 1 minute. Add the mango, pineapple, and avocado and continue blending another minute, until completely smooth. Chill and serve cold.

- 2 cups packed moringa leaves or fresh spinach
- 1 cup full-fat or light coconut milk
- 1 cup Baobab Fruit Drink (page 308)
- 1 cup coarsely chopped mango
- 1 cup coarsely chopped pineapple
- 1 cup coarsely chopped avocado

TROPICAL
BAOBAB SMOOTHIE

SERVES
4

This creamy dairy-free smoothie will take you right to the sun-drenched beaches of Casamance.

» Combine all the ingredients in a blender and purée until smooth and creamy. Serve immediately.

- 2 cups frozen chopped banana
- 1 cup chopped fresh pineapple
- 2 cups full-fat or light coconut milk
- 4 cups Baobab Fruit Drink (page 308)
- ½ cup raw cashew nuts (optional)

SENEGALESE SPOTLIGHT:

Esteval Juices

Growing up in Senegal, the only place to have local juice was at home when you made it yourself. Thus, during recent trips, I was pleasantly surprised to find that hibiscus, tamarind, *ditakh*, baobab, and other local juices have found their way to local supermarket shelves. Cofounded by Valerie Ndiaye, a Senegalese medical doctor, a new local brand, Esteval, was born.

As a doctor, Valerie found that the Senegalese don't consume nearly enough fresh fruits in season, which is especially problematic in light of how damaging vitamin and mineral deficiencies can be in women and children. Like the monks of Keur Moussa (see page 268), she became aware of the abundance of fruits that go to waste after harvest. These observations, combined with the absence of local products in stores that are instead invaded by imported beverages full of sugar and artificial ingredients, led her and her partner Stephane Quenum to the solution of bottling local juice. Their products contain no chemicals, artificial flavorings, or coloring. The fruits, which are supplied by fruit growers and producers' cooperatives in regions all over Senegal, are carefully selected to assure the highest quality. Their hope is to not only introduce the tropical fruit flavors of Senegal around the world, but to also create jobs and opportunities for Senegalese fruit producers at home.

ACKNOWLEDGMENTS

As the Wolof saying goes, "Ku Liim Juum" (roughly translates to "he who attempts to name everybody forgets some"). Attempting to remember everyone who contributed to this book will open the door to many omissions.

To my publisher Hiroko Kiiffner and her husband Cal, I am greatly indebted to you for having believed in me and inspiring me to take on this challenge (and many others).

I am ever grateful to my family, my life partner Umaimah and our three children Sitoë, Elijah, and Haroun, who patiently push me every step of the way. Without your unwavering support and encouragement, this book would never have been written. You are my rock. I love you!

To Jenn Sit, a true gem to collaborate with during the writing of this book. This book is hers as much as it is mine.

To Evan Sung, for capturing the beauty of Senegalese food culture through his lens.

To Laura Palese, whose gorgeous design graces the pages of this book.

To my indefatigable aunt, Marie Mathiam, and her daughter Amsi who graciously opened their homes to my hungry crew, patiently endured the lights of the projectors and the scrutiny of the cameras, and beyond a doubt, served us the best meals we had while making this book.

To my sister Gina, who efficiently covers for me during my frequent travels.

To all my friends who helped coordinate the logistics of my many trips to Senegal: Ely Paul Biagui, Simon and Arlette Boulos, Yacine Dansokho, Amadou Arame and Fatou Diagne, Marielle Dieng, Didier and Jeanine Diop, Dior Fall, Laurence Gavron, Rama Gaye, Ali Baba Gueye, Omi and Monique Kande, Jean Michel and Aida Mathiam, Bouba Mbaye, Benoit and Fatou Bintou Sambou, Jean Pierre and Marie Claude Senghor, and Abba (the Diola from Spain).

To chef Mame Awa Hughes and her husband.

To chef Hamidou Dabré, who is never too far from me in the kitchen.

To the AfroEats team, Ibrahima Basse, Fati Ly, Fatou Mboup, Bibi Seck, Aida (Dada) Thiam, Valerie Ndiaye, and Rama Gaye.

To chef Ali Baba Gueye and to DJ/chef Tamsir Ndir in Dakar.

To chefs Anita Lo, Christian Abegan, Dave Arnold, Samuel Beket, Abdoul Gueye, Eric Simeon, and Alexander Smalls, who accompanied me in Senegal.

To Jessica Harris, for her pioneering role in spreading the word on our cuisine.

To my friend Dr. Marco Polo Hernandez, whose body of work opened my eyes to Africa in Mexico.

To Moussa "Pitié" Diadhiou and Moustapha Barry, for their priceless cultural and food memories of Casamance.

To Gary and Einav for their constant encouragement.

To Ogo Sow (Mr. Africa) and the ATA team.

To the Bergman family, staunch supporters of African cuisine.

To Mieko and Takao Ikegame.

To Mamadou Niang, for his valuable brotherly advice.

To Margot Davis and Anthony L. Browne.

To Drs. Sonia and Jeffrey Sachs and the team at Potou's Millennium Village.

To Dr. Roseline Remans, for her support and work on agriculture, nutrition, and environment.

To Vicky and Pascal Bokar, my San Francisco family.

To the team at the Institut de Technologie Alimentaire (ITA), for their groundbreaking research work on our local food products.

Last, but not least, to the women of African descent who preserve the culinary traditions that inspired this book.

SOURCE GUIDE

The recipes in this book call for ingredients readily available in specialty stores and online. You'll find a selection of sales outlets listed here in alphabetical order.

Adja Khady Food Distributor
This Harlem-based store and wholesale distributor has all the key ingredients that you need to prepare Senegalese food.
243 West 116th Street
New York, NY 10026
Tel. 212-933-0374 or 646-645-7505

Amazon
A convenient online source for ordering a variety of ingredients, including *moringa* powder, broken rice, red palm oil, baobab powder, and *selim* pepper.
www.amazon.com

The Meadow
With two retail stores in Portland, Oregon and one in New York City, the Meadow sells more than 110 artisan salts and a selection of peppers, including *selim* pepper.
www.atthemeadow.com

Odyssey African Market
A Brooklyn-based source for many Senegalese ingredients, including *fonio*.
1124 Fulton Street
Brooklyn, NY 11238
Tel. 718-789-7077 or 718-206-1594

Vitacost
An online source for red palm oil, including the Nutiva and Alaffia brands that both source from small organic family farms.
www.vitacost.com

Yolele Foods
My newly launched line of Senegalese food products sourced from the best of the country's artisan producers.
www.yolelefoods.com

When in Senegal, I rely on the following local sources for staples and specialty ingredients. Some are wholesalers whose products are available in local shops. I recommend that you refer to their websites or email them for further information.

Les Delices De La Mer
The place to go when in need of salted, fermented, and smoked seafood products, the funky ingredients that make Senegalese cuisine so special.
E-mail: Khadycg@yahoo.fr

Esteval
Producer of local juices made from baobab, hibiscus, tamarind, ditakh, ginger, and more.
www.esteval.net

GIE Koba Club Dandemayo
A women-run cooperative and leading fonio producer in Kedougou.
E-mail: kobaclub@gmail.com

MAC-CERF- SN/THS
Joal-based source for salted millet couscous, a specialty of the region, as well as salted, fermented, and smoked seafood products.
E-mail: macha.allah@yahoo.fr

Mor Moringa
Specializes in moringa, baobab powder, baobab oil, and shea butter.
www.mormoringa.com

La Vivriere
Specializes in all the local grains: fonio, all sizes of millet couscous, millet flour, and broken corn.
www.lavivriere.com

Zena
Pioneer and producer of food products made from local ingredients, including juices, syrups, jams, and other spices and condiments.
www.zenaexoticfruits.com

BIBLIOGRAPHY

Baum, Robert M. "Diola (West Africa)." *The Encyclopedia of Religion and Nature*. London: Bloomsbury, 2005. Print.

Brüntrup, M., T. Nguyen, and C. Kaps. "The rice market in Senegal." *Agriculture & Rural Development* 1/2006: 22-25.

Chadare FJ, AR Linnemann, JD Hounhouigan, MJ Nout, and MA Van Boekel. "Baobab food products: a review on their composition and nutritional value." *Critical Reviews in Food Science and Nutrition* 49.3 (2009): 254-74.

Colen, Lisbeth, Matty Demont, and Jo Swinnen. "Smallholder participation in value chains: The case of domestic rice in Senegal." *Rebuilding West Africa's Food Potential*. Food and Agriculture Organization of the United Nations (FAO), 2013.

Essuman, Kofi Manso. "Fermented fish in Africa: A study on processing, marketing, and consumption." Food and Agriculture Organization of the United Nations (FAO), 1992.

Fahey J. "*Moringa oleifera*: A Review of the Medical Evidence for Its Nutritional, Therapeutic, and Prophylactic Properties. Part 1." *Trees for Life Journal*. 2005.

Harris, Jessica B. *High on the Hog: A Culinary Journey from Africa to America*. New York: Bloomsbury, 2012. Print.

Harris, Jessica B. *Iron Pots & Wooden Spoons: Africa's Gifts to New World Cooking*. New York: Fireside, 1989. Print.

Harris, Jessica B. *The Welcome Table: African American Heritage Cooking*. New York: Fireside, 1995. Print.

Jideani IA, and VA Jideani. "Developments on the cereal grains *Digitaria exilis* (acha) and *Digitaria iburua* (iburu)." *Journal of Food Science and Technology* 48 (2011): 251–259.

Kimani, Mary. "Safeguarding Africa's fishing waters." *Africa Renewal* Jul. 2009: 10.

Oguntibeju, OO, AJ Esterhuyse, and EJ Truter. "Red palm oil: nutritional, physiological and therapeutic roles in improving human wellbeing and quality of life." *British Journal of Biomedical Science* 66.4 (2009): 216.

Rizzotto AC, and M. Demont. "Extending reach to strengthen value chains: Increasing consumer awareness of quality Senegal River Valley rice." Presentation at Second Africa Rice Congress, Bamako, Mali, Mar. 2010.

United States Agency for International Development. "Global Food Security Response: Senegal Rice Study." Oct. 2009.

INDEX